Praise for the Book

This book is gold. As you read it, you will inevitably identify with some of the stories and wisdom. You will find yourself reflecting on your own life and career, and getting excited as you glimpse possibilities for playing a much bigger game than the current path you see yourself on.

Brian is truly "a man to cross the river with". He has been a great friend, coach and encourager through the mountains and the valleys, and we have crossed a number of big rivers together over the years. He continues to be a significant influence in expanding my sense of what's possible as a leader.

Dean Phelan, former CEO,
Churches of Christ in Queensland
Board Adviser, CEO Mentor and Executive Coach

Let yourself be captivated by the thoughts, the practical propositions and ... the metaphor of the "Big Kahuna" proposed by Brian Donovan, an expert in game-changing leadership and digital transformation. You will enjoy discovering and reading *Leadership Is Changing the Game.* It will benefit you to shift your mindset, influence others and invent new ways of doing business.

Prof. Yves Pigneur, University of Lausanne
Author with Alex Osterwalder of the international
bestseller *Business Model Generation*
Ranked #7 by Thinkers50 a global ranking
of management thinkers

We can't get to exciting new places without knowing where we want to be, and how to get there. Moving from being a subject matter expert into leadership is an exciting journey, but it is fraught with obstacles. We each need a map for our own personal journey, that helps us honestly identify challenges, including those we create for ourselves, and which equips us to take advantage of opportunities as they arise. Brian helped me make brave decisions to embark on my big life changes. He asks all the right questions and his years of experience and buckets of wisdom are reflected in this great book. It will help *you* to work out how to map *your* own journey, to get there and also to identify how to make a success of your career when it reaches its next destination. Read it!

Kathryn Watt, Non-Executive Director
Former General Counsel, Vanguard Australia

I have worked with Brian to develop my leadership capabilities and his approach has helped me achieve some significant 'game-changing' results. This book captures all the principles and practices that I've used myself. Having these laid out in the book provides a great reference to continually use and refine. With technology and business now inseparable, this book will help technology leaders make game changing impacts to their organisations.

Geoff Spicer, Group General Manager,
Technology & Services, Village Roadshow Ltd

I am honoured to provide this endorsement for Brian Donovan's book *Leadership Is Changing the Game.*

Through this book you will learn to identify the barriers and performance issues that may be holding you back both personally and professionally.

Being an effective leader takes time, desire and hard work. If you are ready to put in the effort, I can assure you that applying the principles within this book will produce positive results.

I highly recommend Brian to others seeking to achieve greatness.

Trent Dean, Head of Clinical Governance,
Royal Flying Doctor Service, Queensland Section

I worked through Brian's executive coaching program and it certainly changed my leadership game. It's great to see the material we covered brought to life in this book. I value the learnings from our work together and particularly the confidence I gained to be the best version of me, so I can now happily take a seat at any leadership table. I am still actively identifying opportunities to change the game and guiding others to do the same. I am glad to have this book to recommend to my team and colleagues and anyone who aspires to be a game-changing leader."

Fi Slaven, General Manager,
William Buck, Victoria

Leadership Is Changing the Game, presents a useful conceptual model for developing leadership potential and ability and provides a wide range of supportive references to credible research and other relevant thought leaders. It includes a valuable and inspirational compilation of actual experiences drawn from Brian's personal career and especially from his successful coaching and team leadership practice.

There's something in this work for everyone, no matter how advanced their leadership experience and journey, but it will be especially helpful for those making the transition from a successful technical role to wider enterprise management and leadership.

Congratulations Brian for a practical, motivational and well researched book.

Gerry Moriarty, AM FTSE FAICD Hon FIEAust
Company Adviser and Director

Every strategic technology executive leverages technology in new and innovative ways to create new customer value, increase margins, and enhance shareholder wealth. The one key common factor in their success is strategic LEADERSHIP. If you are a technology leader who wants to help your company succeed in today's highly competitive marketplace, you need to read *Leadership Is Changing the Game*. It will help you understand *how* leadership is developed and implemented to change the game and improve the competitive position of your company. If you do apply the insights from this book, you will find that you will be highly sought after by businesses as they scramble for strategic leadership. So, don't wait, read the book, and change the game!

Phil Weinzimer, Thought Leader, Consultant,
Speaker and author of *The Strategic CIO: Changing
the Dynamics of The Business Enterprise*

Brian is an inspiring leadership coach who helps aspiring and established leaders to break through situational or ongoing leadership challenges by changing the game.

Brian's style challenges, influences and empowers the individual to get the clarity required to truly grow and prosper.

Brian's book, *Leadership Is Changing the Game* brings to life the principles of his vast leadership and coaching experience in an accessible and applicable manner and represents a must read for any leader in today's high paced and fast changing environment.

Liam Fraser, Director, Singtel Optus

I've been privileged to have been coached by Brian when I took on an executive technology role a number of years ago. Brian had an amazing ability to see things through my eyes, but at the same time he caused me to see my own leadership effectiveness with such clarity and honesty. My only regret is that I didn't get the advantage of being coached by Brian in my earlier leadership roles!

Brian's passion for helping me play a bigger game involved me writing a vision for an amazing future - 'an even bigger game plan'. I recently reflected back on that big game plan and thanks to Brian's support and inspiration, I found the courage to start my own business. Five years on, in the digital strategy work that my firm does, the pivotal success factor is the role that technology leaders play to bring their company's digital strategy to life. Brian's book is a compelling read for technology leaders who want to lead a digital strategy to a successful outcome and change the game for their organisations.

Chris Stevens, Managing Partner,
Digital Frontier Partners

Brian's book is a must read for both business and technology leaders and those with leadership aspirations. He captures the issues and challenges facing leaders in today's ever changing, competitive and disruptive environment. He graphically illustrates the need for collaboration from the Board level strategy, to technical execution and a well-orchestrated change program. The underlying theme being that talent needs to be prepared for leadership with the mentorship of the Board and C-suite executives. Brian neatly shows how individuals in leadership must have a plan, not be afraid to ask for help, and communicate often and broadly.

Denis McGee, Former senior technology executive, with ANZ Bank, NAB and Wells Fargo

This book provides sound and well-tested advice on how to make the transitions from making decisions about technology, to decisions about people, to decisions about the future of your organization. If you apply this book's 'influence curve' to your career, it will guide you on how to refocus your decision making as your audience and scope change.

Prof. Rick Watson, University of Georgia Research Director for the Advanced Practices Council of the Society of Information Management

Tiberius Claudius Caesar Augustus Germanicus was the first Roman Emperor from outside of Italy. Because he was afflicted with a limp and slight deafness, he was thought "different". His family and the Roman political elite ostracized him, excluded him from public office, as well as military service.

Like Claudius, technology leaders are also thought of as kind of weird. They come from outside of mainstream business and are often prevented from having "a seat at the table" because they are different.

Claudius proved to be an able and efficient administrator. He was also an ambitious builder, constructing many new roads, aqueducts, and canals across the Empire.

Likewise, when technology leaders are afforded a "seat at the table", they perform exceptionally well. Their exposure to the information technology applications that enables the company to run, gives them a unique holistic understanding of the enterprise. They are critical thinkers by vocation and masters of the digital world, the future of business, where value is created in moving electrons instead of moving atoms. However, the key to their success is leadership.

Both technology leaders and the businesses they serve need the wisdom offered by Brian in his new book. Technology leaders for the seasoning and polish needed to move from excelling at what they do into helping others excel at what they do. Businesses can benefit from knowing how to develop and leverage the technology leaders in their midst, that they so desperately need now and into the future.

Dr James Stikeleather, University of South
Florida, Muma College of Business.
Formerly Chief Innovation Officer for Dell and the
Chief Technology Officer for Perot Systems

I was initially sceptical about the value that coaching could provide when I was first offered the opportunity to work with Brian. I had never done anything like it before. However, the outcome for me was priceless.

It helped me to grow both personally and professionally. I knew how to produce results on my own. But it was a huge breakthrough for me to step up my leadership and get much bigger results through people. Brian helped me build my leadership influence so that I could impact the big strategic challenges that our business faces.

This book is full of the practical insights and stories that Brian brought to our work together. It serves as a reminder to me to continue to play a big game. If you are a leader looking for the satisfaction of making a big difference then let this brilliant book guide you.

Sarit Cohen, Regional Vice-President and Customer Engagement Manager for APAC, Amdocs

Leadership Is Changing the Game

LEADERSHIP IS CHANGING THE GAME

The Transition from Technical Expert to Leader

Brian Donovan

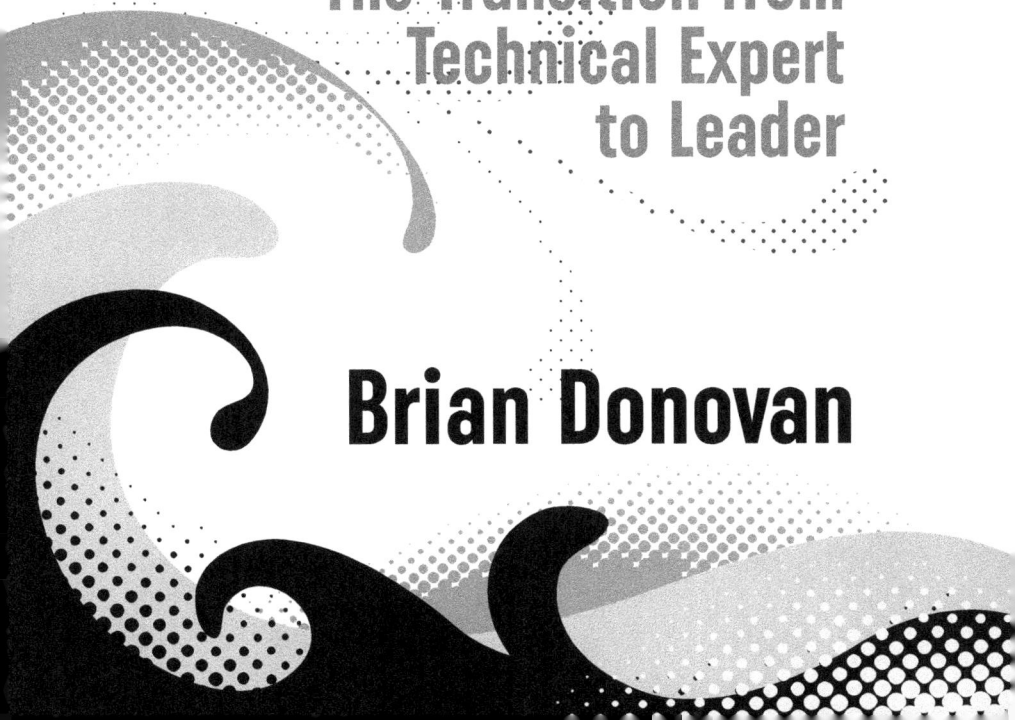

Published by Donovan Leadership
PO Box 536
Camberwell VIC 3124
Australia
www.donovanleadership.com

DONOVAN
LEADERSHIP

Typeset by BookPOD

Disclaimer
The material in this book is general comment only and neither purports nor intends to be specific advice related to any particular reader. It does not represent professional advice and should not be relied on as the basis for any decision or action on any matter that it covers. To the maximum extent permitted by law, the author and publisher disclaim all responsibility and liability to any person or entity, whether a purchaser or not, in respect to anything and of the consequences of anything done by any such person in reliance, whether in whole or in part, upon the whole or any part of the contents of this publication.

ISBN: 978-0-6482950-0-6 (pbk)
eISBN: 978-0-6482950-1-3 (e-book)

Acknowledgements

I recently reconnected with a former client whom I had not seen in many years. He was eager to tell me how he was still using some of the principles we had covered in my coaching program almost a decade earlier. Back then he was going through a rough patch and was in danger of alienating people around him. He could have reacted with righteous indignation about criticisms being levelled at him — in his mind, he was working his butt off and was not being valued. But his generosity of spirit won the day, and instead he took on the challenge of turning himself into the leader he had always wanted to be. Today he is almost unrecognisable. He now knows himself as someone who has been instrumental in the growth of his business, and as a leader with a vision of how his company's technology can change the world.

I am inspired by his example and by those of the countless other amazing leaders I have had the privilege of working with. Not content with mediocrity, these leaders aim high and are set on big things in life. They are the inspiration for this book. I have drawn from their stories and experiences to illustrate the point that we are all capable of being great leaders if we are willing to step up and play a big game.

While I have had the opportunity to contribute my insights from the side-lines, it is these leaders who are on the field doing the work. I would not be able to make a difference as a coach and facilitator without their commitment to changing the game in their sphere of influence. My insights, feedback and encouragement would be worth little without their willingness to reach into themselves to find a new level in their leadership. I owe a huge debt of gratitude to all those leaders who are making the difference they know they can make. This book is dedicated to them.

This book would also not have happened without the impetus of Thought Leaders Business School and the influence of its principals, Matt Church and Peter Cook, as well as the encouragement of fellow participants and alumni of the program.

Clients and colleagues too numerous to mention have supported me simply by listening to my outline of the book and then urging me to write it. You will never know how much impact your encouragement had.

Just like leadership, writing a book is a team sport. I am blessed to have the love and support of my family. My partner Ruth has believed in me and patiently encouraged me. I am grateful to her for the life we have together and how that has enabled me to do the work I love. I am thankful to my three (adult) children, Craig, Kirsty and Bob, who keep me honest and living a life full of new possibilities — something we have always wanted for each other. A special mention to my friend and colleague Dean Phelan, who has constantly encouraged me even through a period when he faced a life-threatening illness. My thanks to Jem Bates, who has shown me how a brilliant editor can challenge me to think more about you, the reader.

Thank you for picking up this book. People like you who are set on building your leadership capability so that you too can change the game for the better have my utmost respect and admiration. I hope you will use the ideas in these pages to develop your own insights and expand your leadership potential. I wish you every success.

Contents

Part 3: What's Next?

Preface

Leadership is not something you can grasp simply from reading a book. You would not expect to learn how to ride a bike just by reading about it. While some theory may help, you need to experience balance through trial and error. Similarly, leadership can be supplemented by knowledge, but wisdom comes from experience. It is true that many books have inspired my own leadership journey, a number of which I reference in this book. My point is that the benefits that came from those books were a direct result of putting that inspiration into practice.

So why write another book on leadership? Well, I believe that technology leaders can take businesses into a new future, and indeed that they are fundamental to Australia's competitiveness. Technology leaders can also change the world for the better, as several game-changing Australian technology businesses are demonstrating. We need to invest in building the leadership capability of our technology leaders to make the most of the disruptive times we live in.

Businesses have high expectations of their technology leaders but, in my observation, do little to develop their leadership capability. In other professional disciplines, such as sales and marketing or professional services, the business benefit of developing that cohort of leaders is self-evident. It is actually just as clear that businesses that develop strategic leadership capability in their technology leaders will outperform their competitors in the marketplace.

I regularly hear CEOs and C-suite executives complain that technology leaders have a poor grasp of the commercial drivers of the business. But when I ask these same executives what they are doing to lift the capability of their tech leaders, I generally get blank stares or motherhood statements about sending them on a leadership course. In my view, this points to a gap in leadership thinking about the important transition from technical expert to leader. Given how important technology-led strategic transformation is for most businesses, this is surprising.

But it's a two-way street. Technology leaders need to take matters into their own hands, rather than waiting for the day they are recognised for their strategic importance. The personal rewards are significant. My own sense from talking to a range of business leaders is that the market demand for game-changing technology leaders will grow dramatically as the development of new technology itself accelerates. Technology leaders who build their leadership capability will have a competitive edge in the employment market.

In this book, I have attempted to distil many of the lessons I have learned from 40-plus years of working with technical experts transitioning to leadership. In that time, and particularly in the last decade or so as an executive coach, I have noticed that some leaders make a smooth transition from technical expert to leader, but others are held back by the speed bumps they encounter along the way. I have watched brilliant technical minds struggle with moving outside their comfort zone of solving technical problems to face the new challenge of getting results through people. The practical client experiences from my coaching program outlined in this book cover much of what I have learned about what works and what does not on the road to becoming a game-changing technology leader.

I am inspired by the difference that technology leaders can make when they take on a game-changing mindset. In fact, I believe that game-changing leadership is what it's all about. The job of the leader is to *make something new happen* — to take us somewhere we have not been before. To achieve a big objective like that, you have to bring others along with you. This book introduces some practical insights into the actions people have taken to deal with those speed bumps and succeed.

While we might not readily admit it, most of us have experienced self-doubt about whether we really have what it takes to be a game-changing leader. Anyone who has taken on a big objective will be able to relate to this. The examples and stories in this book come from people who have been willing to confront their doubts and find new depths in their leadership. They learned through a mixture of theory and practice, which is the way people learn best.

This is how I hope you will approach this book. You should find plenty of fresh ideas and insights here, but you need to put them into practice to change the game within your sphere of influence. If you are seen as a game-changer, you will gain an edge in the employment marketplace. Just as importantly, you will find the fulfilment that comes from making the difference you know you can make.

I love seeing the light go on for a coaching client when they achieve a result they had previously thought was beyond them. And I would love to hear about what you are taking from this book that helped you on your own leadership journey. If you would like to get in touch, you will find my contact details at the end of the book.

Thank you for being willing to be a game-changing leader. You make a difference.

Introduction

Brett was a great technical expert — so good, a global business asked him to come and work for them. His ability to solve technical problems was highly prized by the business. The clients loved his can-do attitude and how he listened to them to understand their problems and deliver the best solutions. They had grown tired of an unresponsive IT department, and he was like a breath of fresh air. He soon developed a group of advocates in the business.

What they did not know was that he loved solving technical problems. That is why he got into the field in the first place. Even as a kid, he was fascinated by how computers worked. He was always tinkering with technology and pushing the boundaries of what was technologically possible. He loved the intellectual challenge of getting the best from technology.

In fact, he delighted in solving all kinds of problems, whether technical or not. Waiting in line at the supermarket checkout, he imagined self-service long before it became a thing. When eating out, he would see ways the restaurant could improve its processes. He sometimes infuriated his wife by jumping in with solutions to problems she shared with him, instead of just listening and understanding. Like all those with superpowers, he came to realise that his problem-solving talents could be both a blessing and a curse.

Meanwhile his employers decided that, with his can-do attitude and loyal fan base, he would be a better choice to run the IT department than the current guy. They were tired of the unresponsiveness of the IT department to the strategic needs of the business. IT seemed to operate in a vacuum, coming up with ideas that interested the head of technology but that had little buy-in from the business.

Brett had seen the problem coming and had tried to persuade his former boss to get closer to their key stakeholders. But the man had no vision and no strategy, and did not involve his team in decision making. In fact, he spent little time listening to his business unit colleagues about their challenges and business objectives.

Now the problems were all Brett's, and the company had high expectations that he would turn things around.

When we sat down to talk, he shared his fear of suffering the same fate as his boss and being moved on in another year or so. Organisations around the globe were regularly replacing their CIOs, and he knew he was now part of an endangered species. So, he desperately wanted to make his mark in his first 90 to 180 days. He needed a quick transition from being a great technical expert to being a great people leader.

He faced a dilemma, though. His loyal fan base expected that he would continue to support them and deliver on the technology challenges he had been working on. But he also knew that he would be judged on his ability to influence the strategic direction of the business. How could he meet both demands on his time?

Whenever he encountered one of his business unit clients they would bail him up to tell him about their latest operational problems. Not wanting to let them down, he would spend time listening and understanding their problems. But he could see that if he continued solving all their technical issues, he would have no time to address the strategic challenges the business faced. He knew he really needed to focus on finding his replacement to do the operational work of solving client problems.

He was candid enough to admit that the problems his clients brought him were fascinating. It was a bit like taking a drug. He could not easily wean himself off the adrenaline rush he got from technical problem solving. Besides, it was sometimes easier to solve the problem than to explain to someone else how to go about it. He consoled himself with the view that it was really hard to find good people.

As we dug further into his thinking, he admitted that solving technical problems was in his comfort zone. When he thought about it, it was that capability that had got him the job as the head of technology, and it seemed a bit strange that he should now give it up. In fact, it made no sense!

But the fate of his former boss was etched into his psyche. He knew that if he did not deliver on the strategic game-changing aspect of his role, then he would eventually suffer the same fate. It was not that easy to address the strategic challenges that the business faced, though. The business units seemed to operate as separate entities, and the company had no overall business strategy to which to link the technology strategy. He spent time with all his key stakeholders, quizzing them on the challenges they faced. Mostly they were concerned about keeping things going the way they had always done, rather than exploring how they could *change* the game.

We created the idea of a big game, a stretch objective that would take him outside his comfort zone. He knew that the objective needed to be achieved in 90 to 180 days so he could make his mark, and that it needed to demonstrate the bottom-line impact that technology could have on the business. Once he had set the stretch objective it suddenly became very clear that he now had a leadership challenge on his hands. He had an objective that he could not deliver on his own. He needed to build his influence in all directions — up to his management and board of directors, sideways to business unit peers, down to his own team, and even outwards to suppliers and customers in the marketplace.

He set a specific and measurable objective that the executive leadership team would approve a game-changing business case and implementation plan in his first 90 days. His 180-day goal was to achieve a significant milestone toward eventual delivery of the program. Once he had committed to it, he knew he had better get to work to deliver on his promise. He also knew that achieving this stretch objective would require him to tap into new leadership capabilities. Just like the time he registered to run a marathon, having put himself on the hook, it was time to get to work.

It was both scary and exciting. Brett talked of other times in the past when making a big commitment had forced him to draw on untapped reserves to deliver on his promise. Setting up in another country was a case in point.

Parenthood is also a classic example of where commitment comes first and knowledge and skills follow.

Now he had a new problem. How could he surround himself with a great team who shared his vision and commitment? How could he build a stellar team to solve the daily operational problems so he was freed up to work on a more strategic objective? He now had a higher order problem: people. To achieve the stretch objective he had set, he knew he needed to influence people and take them with him. And given how much he loved a problem, he knew this was a problem worth his time.

This book is for Brett and anyone like him who wants to change the game.

Perhaps you identify with Brett. You recognise that making the transition from being a great technical expert to being a great leader requires you to reinvent yourself. In some ways, this may seem counterintuitive. You still enjoy technical challenges and the opportunity to satisfy your key stakeholders with your solutions to their problems. You have been rewarded for being a great technical problem solver, but now you confront a different set of expectations. Marshall Goldsmith expressed it aptly in the title of his book, *What Got You Here Won't Get You There.*

As you embrace your new leadership role, it is good to reflect on what leadership is all about. There are many definitions. Everyone has their own favourite. The one I like is that the main role of the leader is to *change the game*. We do need managers to keep things going and to focus on operational excellence, but history abounds with examples of well-managed businesses that are no longer with us because they failed to change the game.

What's in it for you? I believe that once you build your personal brand as a game-changing leader you will be sought after. You will do work you love and make the difference you know you can make. It will get you into your dream role and the big bucks, but more to the point you will find the fulfilment you seek.

PART 1

Why?

ONE

Why change the game?

In my early career, I saw first-hand the impact of disruptive technology as computer-aided design threatened the traditional electronic drafting profession. It would take us on average two weeks to draw a complex electronic circuit diagram by hand. The clients we served were dissatisfied with the lengthy delays and were hungry for the promise of computer-aided design, which could reduce that time to a few days or hours. But the response of senior drafting leaders at the time was, "Nothing will replace the skill of a human being!"

It was a mindset that was blind to the threat and opportunity of technology disruption. In the space of only a few years the entire profession was wiped out by the new technology. Those who identified the opportunity of the disruption embraced the new technology and their careers took off in a new direction. Those in denial shook their heads in disbelief as the world changed around them.

I am sure you will have your own version of this story, whether you have seen a skill-set or a whole company or perhaps an entire industry disappear. History is littered with examples of successful companies that are no longer with us because they underestimated new entrants with game-changing technology.

> **"429 of the original Fortune 500**
> **companies (1955) are no longer in**
> **business today. Adapt or Die"**
> – Vala Afshar, Chief Digital
> Evangelist for Salesforce –

There is little dispute that a digital revolution driven by technology is changing the game for businesses everywhere. Barely a day goes by without a fresh report identifying a new threat or opportunity in the digital revolution. The main conclusion of many of these reports is that businesses need a game-changing digital and technology strategy.

The Digital Vortex, a compelling report released by Cisco and IMD, has some disturbing news about technology disruption. It appears that a "wait and see" mindset still prevails. The survey of 940 business leaders from around the globe predicts that 40 per cent of top industry incumbents (in terms of market share) will be displaced by digital disruption in the next five years.

Despite the clear implications of these findings, however, nearly a third of businesses surveyed continue to take a "wait and see" approach to digital disruption in the hope of emulating their competitors. That is not the kind of leadership to inspire shareholders, let alone clients or employees. It is definitely not the opportunity mindset of an entrepreneur.

Digital disruption requires a game-changing strategy. And a game-changing strategy demands *game-changing leadership*. It requires an opportunity mindset, as exemplified by the entrepreneurs who are leading the disruption.

Technology disruption is like a huge wave. In the 1970s the "Big Kahuna" was the gun surfer who rode the giant waves. Successful businesses will depend on leaders who know how to ride the wave of accelerating technology disruption.

There has been relatively little discussion about whether businesses have the game-changing leadership capability they need to transform their business. Yet only game-changing leaders can successfully develop and execute a digital and technology strategy, and turn it into an opportunity for business growth.

Over the past few years, we at Donovan Leadership have surveyed the market to try to understand how leaders at all levels could be better developed to become activists in technology-led strategic transformation. The Big Kahuna Leadership Survey is our attempt to understand the market's view of whether we have the leadership capability we need to both address the challenge and capture the opportunity of the digital and technology revolution. We ask influential leaders how businesses can develop the game-changing leadership capability that is needed to meet the challenge of digital disruption. We conduct this survey to stimulate a wider conversation on this critical topic.

In the latest Big Kahuna Leadership Survey in 2016, we asked 47 influential business leaders to consider their leadership capability at three levels — board, C-suite and technology leadership. We posed the following questions:

- How could we better develop boards and C-level executives to become activists for technology-driven strategic transformation?

- How could we build greater leadership capability in technology leaders — our CIOs, CTOs, CDOs, for example?

Big Kahuna survey results — a wake-up call for leaders

In the 2016 survey, with the assistance of Andrews Group, a research and strategy consultancy, we conducted qualitative, in-depth interviews with participants with various job titles, including board members, Chief Executive Officers, C-suite executives, Chief Information Officers, academics and consultants. Figure 1 shows a breakdown of the position titles of the respondents.

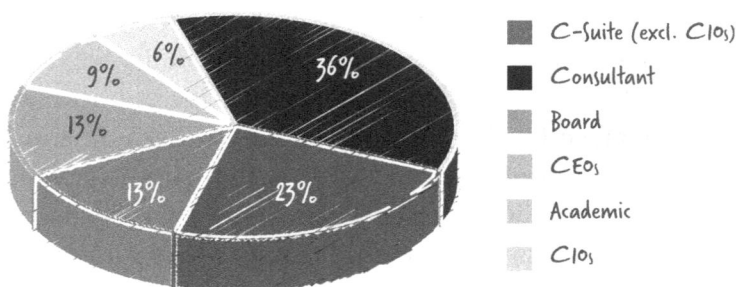

Figure 1: The Big Kahuna Leadership Survey 2016 — breakdown of respondents

The participants represented a broad range of industries, including banking, energy, government, recruitment, telecommunications, finance, education and transport. A wide spectrum of business sizes was also represented, from self-employed consultants to organisations with annual turnovers up to $1.5 billion.

Despite the diversity of the respondent group, there was a high degree of unanimity among the respondents across the lines of enquiry explored in the research. The combined high diversity and high unanimity suggests the findings of this study are relevant to all organisations in all sectors.

The results provide a wake-up call for businesses to better understand their company-specific view of their leadership capability.

The respondents were well tuned to the message they have heard from myriad reports that they need a well-considered strategy to address the challenge and opportunity of digital and technology disruption. But there was broad agreement that the current level of leadership is insufficient for the challenge of developing and executing a successful digital or technology strategy.

Those companies that develop game-changing leadership capability, the survey results indicate, will be better equipped to embrace the future.

Digital disruption provides significant opportunities for growth. For example, evidence suggests that those companies whose technology leaders are actively involved in business strategy outperform their peers by a margin of almost two to one. This is a compelling argument for a more strategic role for CIOs, CTOs and those in similar leadership roles. So why isn't it happening more often? A recent global report indicated that a lack of leadership or digital talent tops the list of hurdles to implementing a successful digital program.

The challenge and opportunity of digital disruption is real. But how it might affect your business is hard to predict and harder to plan for.

The main conclusion of the survey is that technology leaders need to move up the influence curve. Boards and C-suite executives are acutely aware that technology is likely to disrupt their businesses over the next three to five years. They are urgently looking to technology leaders to provide them with strategic guidance on how to both avoid the threat and capitalise on the opportunities of this next wave of disruption.

Put bluntly, they are not seeing technology leaders giving the level of advice needed to bring digital and business strategies together. When I present these findings to groups of technology leaders, their response is often, "It's not us, it's them!" In other words, the business doesn't know what they want; it doesn't understand the challenge of supporting legacy systems and is unwilling to invest in innovation. While there is a case to be made that all C-suite executives need a good grasp of technology, we may not be able to change their outlook in the short term. However, technology leaders can change how they respond to the challenge.

It is alarming that we are not doing more to build the leadership capability of technology leaders. What should concern us is that the predictable future if nothing changes, and if we cling to the mindset of "It's not us, it's them", is a loss of competitive edge for businesses and a loss of economic value creation for Australia as a nation.

Current leaders are often ill equipped to handle, or even think about, digital disruption. The key, therefore, is to develop the leadership capability to embrace complexity and respond creatively while remaining grounded in today's business disciplines.

I strongly recommend that businesses undertake a critical evaluation of the current level of leadership capability. A diagnostic review will indicate areas for improvement.

To drive the success of your business in the challenging times ahead, a company-specific assessment needs to be based on two key factors. The first is whether leaders at all levels are actively generating a vision of what is possible for the business through technology-led strategic transformation.

The second factor to assess is whether leaders can elicit strong ownership of the future from within the organisation — in other words, are they bringing people along with their vision and strategy?

The model in figure 2 illustrates the game-changing outcome of getting those two ingredients to match. It also highlights the consequences of falling short on one or both of these two factors.

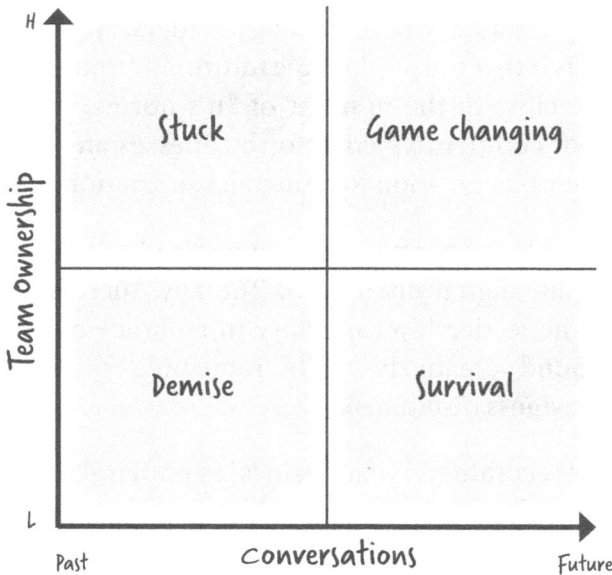

Figure 2: Key success factors for strategic transformation

The Big Kahuna Leadership Survey results indicate that there are opportunities at all three levels of company leadership (figure 3). Boards can enhance their technology input and influence digital strategy. Technology-literate CEOs and C-suite executives will have an appetite for technology-led strategic transformation. Technology leaders (CIOs, CTOs etc.) can influence the strategic and business focus of organisations.

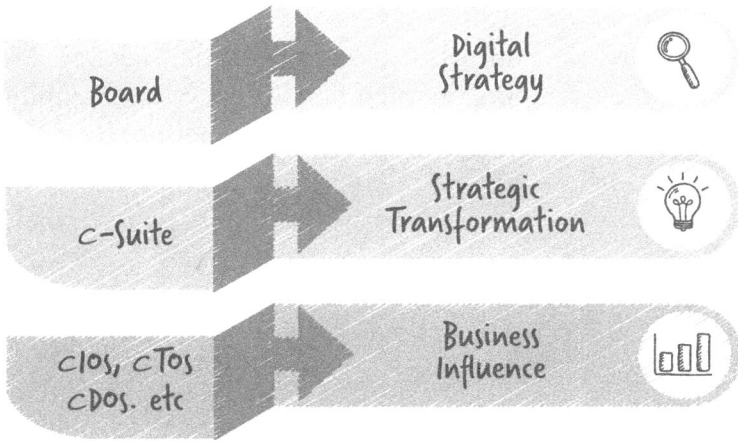

Figure 3: Leadership diagnostic

The following are some relevant concerns at each leadership level:

- **Board.** Is the board asking the right questions about technology strategy? Does the board need to enhance its technology input to be better able to influence digital strategy? For example, some businesses have established a technology and digital business advisory panel to advise the board on "strategic application of new technologies".

- **C-suite.** What is the level of technology literacy of your CEO and C-suite executives, and do they have the appetite for technology-led strategic transformation? Do they have the game-changing leadership capability to share their vision and gain organisational ownership for its adoption?

- **Technology leaders (CIOs, CTOs, CDOs etc.).** Are your technology leaders shifting from an IT operational focus to a customer and business focus? Are they futurists or merely order takers? Are they stepping up the influence curve to champion technology-led strategic transformation?

TWO

Why be a game-changing leader?

Build your brand as a game-changing leader

Leanne inherited a poisoned chalice when she took on her new role. Her new employer, a global technology services business, had lost the confidence of a major client. Her job was to rebuild what had become a toxic relationship. It was a multimillion-dollar account and the client's perception of her employer was at an all-time low. Attempts at conciliation had turned into threats of legal action.

All eyes were now on Leanne to turn things around.

She committed to the objective of restoring the relationship in the next six months. Sensibly, she aligned her team on the objective. There were plenty of naysayers who insisted it could not be done, but she would give it her best shot. She took responsibility for the client's perception of her employer and presented a plan that would provide the client with the value she believed was missing. And she asked for and received support from her global leadership team.

It was not long, however, before her little voice of doubt kicked in. "Who are you kidding? You don't have what it takes to deliver on your promise," it told her. This kind of self-doubt had dogged her throughout her career. Whenever the stakes were raised she knew this conversation would kick in. If we are honest, every one of us could identify with her, especially when we have made a big commitment. Leanne thanked her little voice for sharing and started a new, bigger conversation about putting the client at the centre of the universe.

The results she and her team produced spoke volumes. Through her ability to listen to the client's problems and address them in a committed way, Leanne achieved the complete turnaround she had aimed for. Key stakeholders in the client organisation began to sing her praises.

She began to build a personal brand as the turnaround person and has since been promoted and given more challenging turnaround assignments. Her reputation in the marketplace has grown, and she has been headhunted for exciting assignments that she is now evaluating.

Leanne confronted her demons to avert a significant risk for her business. She changed the game for them. Of course, game-changing leadership is not for everyone, and it is certainly not for the faint-hearted. It takes courage and commitment. Because there is no formula to follow, it is never comfortable. But for leaders like Leanne it is ultimately more fulfilling than playing it safe.

I believe that leaders who produce game-changing results will be in increasing demand. The market feedback in the latest Donovan Leadership Big Kahuna Leadership Survey supports this view, particularly as businesses seek to execute strategies to avert the risk or capture the opportunity of technology disruption.

Are you considering building your brand as a game-changing leader? Yes, it is riskier than playing it safe, but ultimately it is way more rewarding. Let's talk about playing it safe.

Playing it safe is not that safe

Amazon failed with its attempt to introduce a cool smartphone, Fire Phone. The hotel booking site Amazon Destinations was another epic failure. Amazon Auctions and several other ventures crashed and burned. Jeff Bezos, Amazon's CEO, believes failed experiments are a necessary evil to creating successful inventions. He sees failure and inventions as "inseparable twins".

Some of Amazon's bold bets, such as Amazon Web Services, are paying off big time. The launch of Amazon in Australia may be another bold bet. Amazon is doing well in the USA and UK, but struggling in France and Canada. If Australian businesses are hoping to see them off as they did Borders bookstores, though, they may be disappointed. There is plenty of strategic advice being offered about how to be "Amazon-ready" both to avert the threat and to capture the opportunity their arrival offers.

But what about the game-changing leadership that is required to be "ready" for Amazon, or indeed any other disruptors? What can we learn from Amazon itself about their approach to leadership? The first thing to note is that the topic is important enough for Amazon to publish its own set of 14 leadership principles.

One of these principles may help explain Jeff Bezos' views about failure.

Invent and Simplify

Leaders expect and require innovation and invention from their teams and always find ways to simplify. They are externally aware, look for new ideas from everywhere, and are not limited by "not invented here". Because we do new things, we accept that we may be misunderstood for long periods of time.

– Extract from Amazon leadership principles –

In a letter to shareholders, Jeff Bezos said, "To invent you have to experiment, and if you know in advance that it's going to work, it's not an experiment. Most large organizations embrace the idea of invention, but are not willing to suffer the string of failed experiments necessary to get there."

Experimentation and risk are not without context, however. Clarity about what it is you are trying to achieve — the big problem you are trying to solve for your customers — is the critical reference point for experimentation and pressing on in the face of failure. You have to know what you want, and to be prepared to try many different ways to get there, learning as you go...until you make a breakthrough.

In his book, *Taking Smart Risks*, Doug Sundheim suggests leaders need to reframe risk. Instead of merely focusing on what can go wrong, he proposes that we consider what we have to lose by avoiding risk. He identifies five common dangers of playing it safe for too long:

- You don't win.
- You don't grow.
- You don't create.
- You lose confidence.
- You don't feel alive.

Game-changing leaders are passionate about making a positive difference and are prepared to risk failure to get there. Are you willing to take smart risks and be a game-changing leader?

Game-changing leadership is the key for the new superstars who are disrupting the business landscape.

How can you emulate the superstars?

MIT recently announced their annual list of the 50 Smartest Companies. These superstar companies made the list because they demonstrated an especially impressive combination of technological leadership and business acumen, as judged by MIT, over the past year. What can we learn from these superstar businesses?

David Rotman, the editor of *MIT Technology Review*, suggests "they got there through exploiting a growing gap in digital competencies...and have gained their power at least in part by adeptly anticipating and using digital technologies".

But what can we learn about leadership from these superstar businesses? Jensen (Jen-Hsun) Huang, CEO of graphics chip maker Nvidia, may not be as well-known as Jeff Bezos at Amazon or Elon Musk at Tesla, but he is ranked number six in HBR's list of Best-Performing CEOs in the World. And Nvidia tops MIT's list of smartest companies.

Huang believes the biggest challenge for any business is reinvention. "Every successful thing needs to be torn down and rebuilt at some point. It is challenging, takes courage and is gut wrenching," he says. Clearly equilibrium is not an option for Huang. Nvidia is now establishing itself as the leading provider of processing power for AI software, and its newer AI-related businesses are growing quickly.

How could you emulate Huang's game-changing leadership and the courage it takes to tear down the old and rebuild it? Is this the difference between leadership and management?

Leadership vs management

At its peak in the late 1980s, Digital Equipment Corporation (DEC) had $14 billion in sales and 130,000 employees, and was ranked among the most profitable companies in the US. DEC's founder and CEO, Ken Olsen, was named by *Fortune* magazine as "the most successful entrepreneur in the history of American business". On four separate occasions the company tried to transition from its traditional minicomputer business into personal computing. Each attempt failed. In 1998 DEC was acquired by Compaq in a fire sale.

As Clayton Christensen puts it in his book, *The Innovator's Dilemma*, DEC's transitioning attempts failed because of a culture clash with the company's traditional minicomputer business. Used to 50 per cent gross profit margins or more, they simply did not understand this new low-margin line of business.

DEC's demise also illustrates the essential difference between leadership and management. It was a very well-managed business. But Olsen was incapable of providing the game-changing leadership to spin off a separate business to pursue the new market they were well placed to go after.

Management is about keeping things going. Leadership is about changing the game. Businesses need both. Good governance and sound processes are essential. However, it is not enough to stay viable as the market changes, as the DEC example illustrates.

We need game-changing leaders who are willing to continually reinvent their organisations and themselves in order to take us somewhere new.

After Steve Jobs returned to Apple in 1997 he provided three examples of the principles of game-changing leadership:

1. He averted a risk they faced by reducing Apple's range of 15 desktop computers to just four, which pulled Apple back from the brink of bankruptcy.

2. He added new value with the introduction of the first iPod, which put 1000 tunes in your pocket.

3. He built on a strength that Apple already had with sleek design, beautiful interfaces and ease of use.

You can apply these principles and change the game within your sphere of influence.

Of course, the problems you face as a leader are not the same as those you once faced as a technical expert.

What is a problem worth your time?

Productivity experts can help you use your time more effectively, but only you will know the answer to the question, "What is a problem worth my time?"

When a client of mine asked himself this career-defining question, he knew at once that one problem worth his time was to dramatically improve his client relationships. Graeme was leading a major project and his stakeholders were upset about expected delays in delivery.

Graeme was well known for producing elegant solutions to complex technical problems. He had a reputation as the go-to person on all manner of technology problems that his department faced. He had been fascinated by technical problems since he was young. Indeed, it was what got him interested in a career in IT. He now realised, however, that his problem-solving superpower must be reinvented. He knew his personal brand as the go-to person needed to change if he was to solve his stakeholder problem and be seen as executive leadership material.

It soon became clear to him that he needed a great team delivering results to succeed in his quest. If the current project was not on track, his clients would not even talk to him about their future objectives.

That led him to alter some of the practices he used with people around him. When they brought problems to him, he pressed *them* for recommendations. He asked more questions instead of being drawn into providing answers. And he made many more requests of his team. As he stepped up his leadership, he reinvented his strength and became more interested in how to get other people to solve problems.

Graeme and his team did turn things around and his stakeholders became some of his best advocates. Word soon spread about his new personal brand. In a strange turn of events, one of his key stakeholders was promoted to another business and asked him to join her there. She knew he was the perfect person to turn around a similar stakeholder issue in her new organisation.

We could all benefit from carving out time for reflective thinking in the way Graeme did. In the HBR article *How to Regain the Lost Art of Reflection* the authors recommend the following practices:

- Schedule unstructured thinking time.

- Get a coach. (True!)

- Cultivate a list of questions that prompt reflective thought.

- Protect yourself and your organisation from information overload.

- Reimagine yourself as a meta-problem solver.

- Be a role model for your employees.

What is a problem worth your time?

PART 2

How?

THREE

Moving up the influence curve

As a leader, you know you can't do it all yourself. The key is to motivate and elicit results from others, and for that you need the so-called soft skills of emotional intelligence to influence those around you. As you develop your ability to influence others, so your leadership potential grows exponentially. That's why it is so important to understand the stages of the influence curve.

Many of us started our career as a subject matter expert. It was all about solving technical problems and growing your expertise in a specialty area, for example as a technology expert, lawyer, accountant or medical specialist. You build a reputation as a great problem solver. Very often the reward for being a great technical expert is to be promoted into leadership.

Once you move above the line into leadership it's all about producing results through people, and you do that through building your influence. As a technical expert, it was about solving the problems; now it's about influencing others to produce bigger results.

As a leader, you need to learn how to influence people in all directions around you. You need to influence your management to support your proposals. Equally you need to influence your business unit colleagues to allocate resources and take them along with you, and to inspire your team to step up their leadership. And your influence may need to extend outside your organisation to your vendors and strategic partners.

It's not enough to make incremental steps in building your influence. Figure 4 charts the stages of influence as an exponential curve to keep pace with the acceleration of technological change. After you have understood each stage and applied it to your own experience, you will be able to see where you are now and where you need to be, given the leadership challenges you face.

This is not something you do just once. You may move up and down the influence curve numerous times in your career. A new job takes you back to the start again, or perhaps a new boss arrives and you need to re-establish yourself. Sometimes the environment around you is completely changed by a reorganisation or a shift in customer expectations. The point is you do not experience the influence curve as a steady upward journey to a finite destination. In leadership you are never done.

The stages of influence I introduce in this book are based on my observations of leaders over several decades. As you move up the influence curve you multiply your leadership potential and your ability to influence others. This is not a handbook of theoretical techniques and tips to follow, however. It's about trying things out so the actual experience of building your influence seeps into your bones.

It would be a mistake to read the book from cover to cover then put it down and say okay, I've got all that. The book is designed around a coaching model I have used successfully with hundreds of business leaders. The coaching program combines theory and practice, which the research shows is how we learn best. You will get results from this model only by putting it into practice, so think of this book as an introduction to the coaching program.

The first step is to examine the stages of the influence curve and determine your own position on it. As already noted, you may have been up and down this curve several times already, or you may be thrust into leadership for the first time. You may find you are currently at one point of the influence curve but recognise that at another stage of your career you were further up the curve. It doesn't matter. The key is first to identify your current location on the curve.

Let's go through the stages of the influence curve. You'll notice that there is a multiplier that represents your leadership potential at each stage. This is based on my observations of leaders I have seen develop their ability to influence others to produce results. This model is not presented as the only 'truth', but rather as one way of representing how leaders can build their leadership potential.

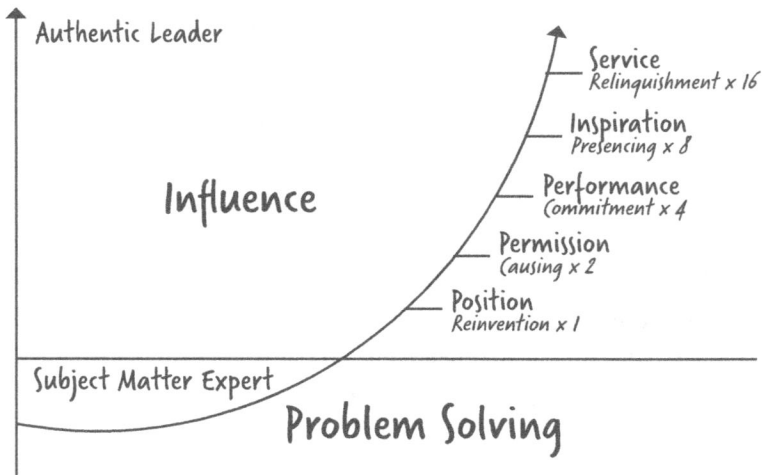

Authentic Leader

Influence

Subject Matter Expert

Problem Solving

Service
Relinquishment x 16

Inspiration
Presencing x 8

Performance
Commitment x 4

Permission
Causing x 2

Position
Reinvention x 1

Figure 4: The influence curve

If leadership is all about changing the game, then by definition there will always be new challenges and new frontiers to explore. We will need to continually find new reserves in our leadership potential.

In the chapters that follow we will explore each stage of the influence curve in turn.

FOUR

Position: Reinvent your strength to change the game

At the position stage on the influence curve (figure 5), the focus is on *reinvention*. By reinvention, I mean taking your inherent strength to a new level.

You are congratulated on securing a new job. You have an impressive position title and a business card you can hand out to people. Unless you now reinvent your inherent strength, though, you will have little or no influence. If all you have is the position title, you're not going to get very far.

If, for instance, your great strength is as a problem solver, reinvention will mean meeting the people problem of getting other people to solve problems! And that higher order problem is one you will spend your entire career working on and still not have mastered when you retire.

Leaders at this level accelerate their leadership potential x 1. Without reinvention, you have little or no influence.

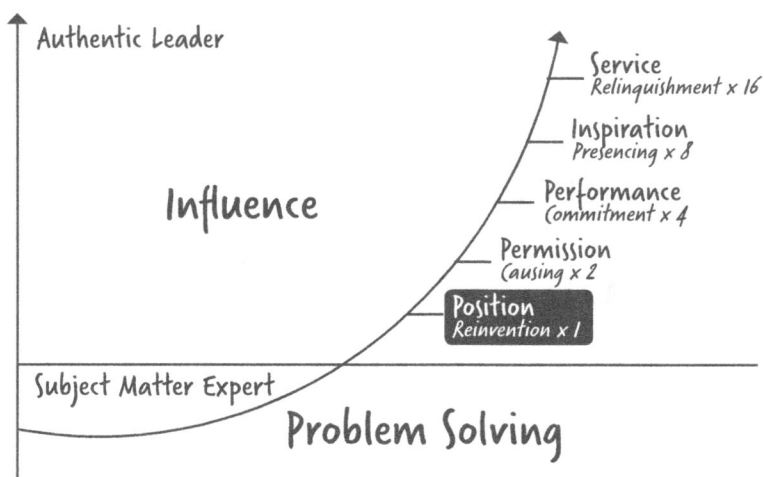

Figure 5: Position stage on the influence curve

No doubt you have seen it happen to others. Having landed the new job, they assumed it came with the authority to get things done. They believed other people should now simply do their bidding. But even in the military, with its much more hierarchical style of organisation, experienced leaders will insist you cannot rely on your command authority alone. To lead successfully, you must be able to bring people along with you.

The challenge with reinventing our inherent strength is that most of us have no idea what it is. We could talk for hours about our weaknesses, but often spend little time on our strength. Yet it is our strength that got us to where we are, and our strength that will take us to the next level once we have reinvented it.

Let's say, for example, your inherent strength is in problem solving, as is true for many in the technology sector. You got into a technical career because you love a problem.

Your strength came to be applied in a narrow specialty area, yet your inherent ability to solve problems runs like a thread through your whole career.

Steve was a great problem solver. In fact, he was originally attracted to a career in the technology sector because he loved solving problems. He soon became a legendary technical expert. Give him a problem and he would work night and day to solve it. He was so good that they made him a leader.

His transition from technical expert to leader was not so smooth, however. It just seemed to Steve like it was quicker to continue to solve many of the complex technical problems himself. He could usually see the solution right away. Besides it took too long to explain it to his team, and it was really hard to get good people. It was not long before he was too busy and feeling overwhelmed.

Steve knew something needed to change or his health would suffer. He was not serving his team or himself by taking on the detailed technical problems. As a leader, he had a higher order problem, which was how to get the best out of people — that was a problem worth his time. He had to reinvent his inherent problem-solving strength.

However, as in many areas of life, it is one thing to come to recognise that something has to change, but quite another to put it into practice. Erica Ariel Fox's book, *Winning from Within* calls this "closing your performance gap". For Steve's reinvention to be successful, he needed to build muscle in how to get results through other people. The practice he adopted was to make specific requests of people around him.

Steve learned the power of making a request for a specific result by a specific time. Pretty soon, people around him started to step up instead of grumbling about him micromanaging them. He also started to free up time in his diary, which allowed him to build game-changing strategies.

If reinventing your inherent strength is a foundation stone for game-changing leaders, making specific requests of others is the practice that turns that concept into reality.

Where could you make requests of others and provide them with a leadership opportunity?

Influence is about you, not your position title or whether you have a seat at the table.

A seat at the table

You often hear leaders say they need a seat at the main leadership table, but if you win that seat, you need to know what to do with it.

You will surely have been to leadership team meetings where some people speak and everyone else listens. On the other hand, you will have seen the opposite occur, where some people speak and no-one listens. I know I have.

I once presented to a leadership group in which there was no sign of any great commitment to the topic. Suddenly one member of the team who had been very quiet spoke up in support of my call for action — and when he spoke, everyone listened. When he recommended they get behind the proposal the whole mood of the meeting changed to positive support. His ability to influence those around the table was remarkable.

How do you build the kind of influence that wins you a seat at the table? Clearly this is not simply a matter of following someone else's formula —quite the opposite, in fact. The key is that it needs to be authentically you.

In his book, *Authentic Leadership*, Bill George says, "Authentic leaders...lead with purpose, meaning and values. They build enduring relationships with people. Others follow them because they know where they stand."

One way to capture where you stand and to build your influence is to enshrine your values in a personal charter. This is an exercise that can help give you clarity about what's important to you. Some questions to consider are:

- What do I stand for?
- What can I be counted on for?
- What values are important to me?

Of course, writing a charter and making it visible for yourself is not the end of the story. You need to put it into practice. It is easy to forget your values and what you stand for when times are stressful. But a personal charter can remind you who you really are — and help you to earn a seat at the table.

Here are some questions to guide your thinking about your personal charter. (We'll return to these in the practical exercises in chapter 10.)

- What is my strength and how could I reinvent it?

- What is my experience as I use my key strength?
- What do others experience when I am using my strength?
- What difference does my strength make in the world?
- As I use my strength, what would I be doing, saying and feeling, and what would be happening around me?
- What daily practices do I have to utilise more of my strength?
- What does my calendar look like as I reinvent my strength?
- What will I stop doing?
- What practices do I utilise when my strength becomes a weakness?
- What conversations could I end to use more of my key strength?
- What conversations could I start to use more of my key strength?
- What can I be counted on for?
- What do I stand for?

The key to keeping your charter alive once you have crafted it is to develop practices. A practice is not simply a concept; it is something you see yourself actually doing. For example, "I will be more accessible to my team" is a concept; "I will schedule between 10.00 am to 12.00 pm each Monday for conversations with team members" is a practice. Practices build muscle on what is inevitably an aspirational charter. For it to be inspiring there has to be an element of aspiration in it. In other words, you have not mastered the values you stand for. Just when you think you have them mastered, something will come along to challenge you. It is easy to forget your values and what you stand for when times are stressful. A personal charter will help keep you on track.

Some companies are adopting the practice of circulating the personal charters or mission statements of their key executives. While I can see the value of a public declaration as a way of keeping you honest, it's up to you to decide what is best shared. The important take-out is that you will be judged by your actions, not your intentions.

An experience with a CEO client gave me a good example of closing this perception gap. He considered himself to be a 'collaborative' kind of a guy. The 360-degree feedback he received did not support his view, though. When he drilled down a bit further into the feedback, what he discovered was that despite his willingness to collaborate, his team could see that his mind was already made up. The collaboration was actually a sham.

The starkest illustrations of the gap between actions and intentions are found in political life. Political leaders no doubt have great intentions, but ultimately voters judge them on their actions.

John Chambers was Global CEO of Cisco for 20 years. People who worked closely with him reported attending customer presentations with him after which he would ask them, "What are three things we could have done better?"

He would listen closely, and next time around he would have integrated the feedback into his presentation.

This was a globally recognised CEO of a Fortune 500 company whose advice was sought by presidents. The markets loved him and he was regularly quoted in the media. He did not need to seek feedback. He could have said, "Don't you know who I am?" But he was always looking to close the gap between his intentions and his actions.

You may believe you understand your key strength, but what's important is how *others* see you. Perception is reality, so we also need to close the gap between how we see ourselves and how others see us.

Close the gap between how you see yourself and how others see you

When I started working for a former boss, he urged me to jump in and tell him what he needed to know. "There are always plenty of people who will tell me what I *want* to hear," he said, "but I want you to tell me what I *need* to hear." To his great credit he was true to his word, and whenever there was something I thought he needed to hear I would remind him of his invitation.

He is not the only leader to have encouraged that kind of contribution, but I have found some others didn't always mean it. What they wanted to hear was how great they are and what a fine job they were doing. It might even be true, but it does not serve us as leaders to be told all the good stuff and nothing about where there might be room for improvement.

How would you rate your driving skills? In a US study, 93 per cent of respondents rated themselves as above-average drivers. In a further survey, 36 per cent of drivers believed they were an above-average driver while texting.

This phenomenon, called illusory superiority, recognises a cognitive bias that causes people to overestimate their positive abilities relative to others'.

Dr Peter Fuda found a similar gap in how leaders judge themselves by their intentions and everyone else by their actions (figure 6). "I've never met a leader who aspires to destroy shareholder value, irritate customers and alienate staff," he explains. "Yet we almost always find a significant gap between a leader's intention and their actual impact."

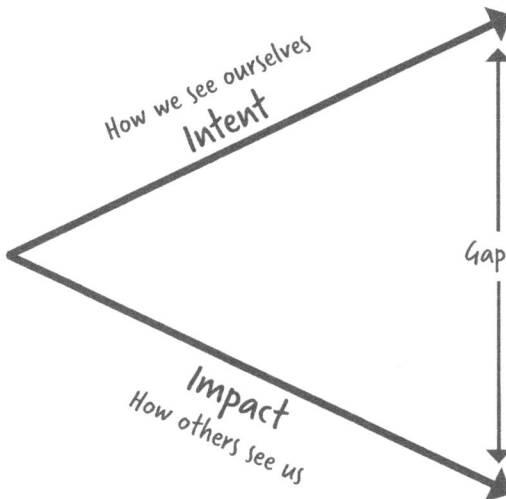

Figure 6: The perception gap

One place we find this bias is in the gap between our capacity to honour our own commitments and what we expect of those around us? As game-changing leaders, we are always making big commitments, and we can only succeed if others do the same. If we are not honouring the small commitments we make along the path to our game-changing objective, then our impact will be reduced no matter how well intentioned we are.

It is so refreshing to work with people who honour their commitments. I love working with Connie for that reason. She manages website updates for me. She always gives a date by which she will complete a task, and she consistently gets it done before the deadline. On the rare occasions when she cannot deliver on her promise, she will let you know as soon as she can and will renegotiate a new date. It is such a contrast to wasting time and energy listening to stories equivalent to "the goat ate my homework"!

If we want more people like that around us, then we need to close the gap between how we see ourselves and how others see us. Otherwise we are like an overweight person giving advice to others about how to lose weight. While it may be valid and well meaning, it lacks authenticity.

One way to close this gap is to ask your key stakeholders directly, do I honour my commitments?

Research by Zenger Folkman concluded that "great leaders are not defined by the absence of weakness, but rather by the presence of clear strengths". In their *Extraordinary Leader* study, they found that leaders with one to three key strengths were placed in the 60th to 80th percentile in their leadership effectiveness.

Maybe at this point you are wondering whether leaders are born or made? I believe everyone has the capacity to be a leader if they commit themselves to the journey.

Are you the same leader you were five years ago?

Or even ten years ago? Of course, you are essentially the same person. But as you continue to confront new challenges, chances are you have also discovered some new depth to your leadership ability, something you did not know you had.

Maybe you pitched yourself at the interview for a big new promotion. When you got the job, you discovered it was way bigger than you had first thought. You may have even privately wondered whether you had what it takes to deliver on your promise. But because of your commitment to succeed, you expanded your leadership capability.

There is a tired old debate about whether leaders are born or made. These lived experiences supported by the research show that leadership is about 30 per cent genetic and 70 per cent learned.

Each time we take on a bigger game, we need a new level of leadership to succeed. It is like adding a second storey to a house — it needs to be solidly underpinned. But what do we need to learn to keep expanding our leadership capability?

A recently published 10-year study found recurring patterns that distinguished exceptional executives from everyone else. One of the key factors revealed in the study was that "they form deep, trusting relationships".

Leaders who are changing the game know they need to continually build their leadership influence. They are constantly expanding their ability to bring people along with them.

How could you expand your leadership influence?

In my experience, one potential obstacle is that we all think we are impostors.

Is impostor syndrome getting in your way?

If you are a game-changing leader, then impostor syndrome could be getting in your way. This is the fear that one day we will be discovered as a fraud.

Faye's experience will illustrate the point. Having impressed her prospective employer at interview, she won a big new job. When she started in the new role and confronted the magnitude of the challenge, she privately questioned whether she really had the capability to deliver on her promise.

Self-help books recommended that she should fake it until she made it. But she needed more than a swagger to save her from sleepless nights listening to her little voice of doubt. Faye unfairly compared herself to the leaders around the table, particularly the men, who appeared to be so confident and to have it all together. All was not as it appeared, though. A recent survey discovered that being found to be incompetent is the number one fear of CEOs and executives worldwide.

Once Faye understood that other leaders were dealing with their own version of self-doubt, she was able to shift her focus to what she was good at. She also gave herself permission to make mistakes. If you are a game-changing leader and the game is big enough, you will occasionally fall short of your objectives. What also comes with the territory is a degree of doubt about your capacity to deliver. In fact, if you have not experienced impostor syndrome, it is likely the game is just not big enough.

Faye put her impostor experience to rest not by trying to make it go away but by focusing on her strengths. She was great at building relationships and connecting with people. It took courage to confront her fears, but she is now able to authentically support people dealing with their own self-doubts and to bring out the best in them. She can now see evidence of her success in her commitment to make a difference.

How could you expand on your strengths and escape impostor syndrome?

In case you still imagine that one day you will reach a point where you stop reinventing yourself, think again. Once you embark on the leadership journey you are *never* done.

In leadership you are never done

In 1996 Alain Passard's Parisian restaurant L'Arpège, was awarded three Michelin stars, denoting "exceptional cuisine that is worth a special journey". In 2001, he completely changed the restaurant's cuisine to make vegetables the centrepiece, a bold move given France's traditional meat-eating culture. Yet he retained his three-star status.

Passard could easily have rested on his laurels, but he was not satisfied with simply repeating a successful formula. In the Netflix series *Chef's Table*, he talks about cooking without recipes. "Next year I don't want to make the same recipes I did last year. When you close your eyes at night, what's important? You've spent the day taking risks. You made some people very happy."

How often do we harbour the illusion that one day we will arrive at leadership nirvana, where we need only keep repeating a tried and proven formula? Even if it were possible, the market could be disrupted at any time, forcing us to search for a new strategy. We could get a new job or a different boss, or key team members could leave. All kinds of things could change around us that would require us to adapt.

As a game-changing leader, you are continually developing yourself to meet the latest challenge.

Research by McKinsey suggests that half of all efforts to transform organisational performance fail either because senior managers don't act as role models for change or because people in the organisation defend the status quo.

My experience with clients is similar. You cannot expect your team members to step up their leadership unless you yourself demonstrate what you demand of them.

One place to start is to seek feedback, not just through the annual 360-degree feedback process, but also via more regular conversations on what we are doing well and what could be improved. You have to be comfortable in your own skin to seek that kind of feedback. You have to be inspired and fulfilled by playing a game in which you are never done.

Where might you seek feedback on what you could do to improve your leadership?

FIVE

Permission: Empower other leaders to step up

Leaders at the permission stage of the influence curve (figure 7) are focused on *causing* great leaders around them.

The breakthrough required at this stage is the ability to "cause" results through others. The ability to cause results is distinct from being a great subject matter expert, where the focus is mostly on being a prodigious *doer*.

Most of us, at some stage in our career, have had the experience of someone believing in us more than we believed in ourselves. While we doubted ourselves, our sponsor, unmoved by our misgivings, believed we would be fine. Usually their faith in us would be rewarded. We would surprise ourselves by finding a new level of leadership ability.

Sometimes you will cause other leaders by holding them to account for their promises or acknowledging their accomplishments. However you do it, the ability to persuade others to step up doubles your leadership potential and produces bigger results.

Leaders at this level accelerate their leadership potential at twice the rate.

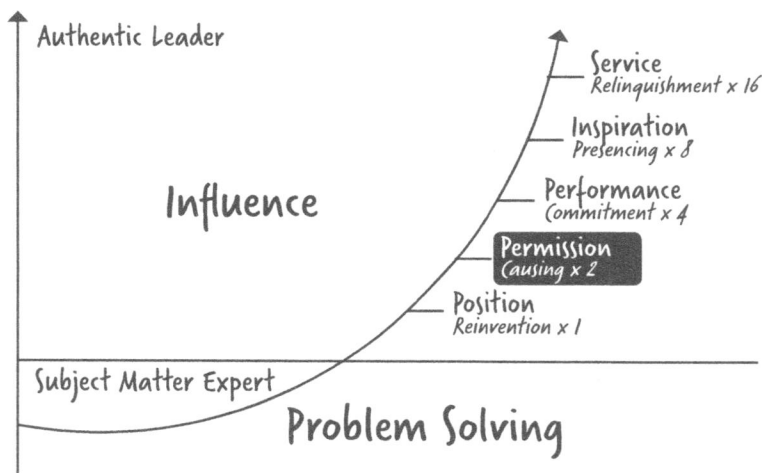

Figure 7: Permission stage on the influence curve

Leaders stand for something

You will recall that I suggested you address the question "What do I stand for?" in your personal charter. The reason for this is that authentic leaders stand for a clear set of values and principles. They also stand for a new future, and for making a difference.

In his TED Talk *How Great Leaders Inspire Action*, Simon Sinek recommends that leaders start with why: *why do you believe what you believe?* He argues that people don't buy what you do as much as why you do it. There is something about the passion we tap into that energises us, and attracts others to want to come and play with us.

- Mahatma Gandhi stood for Indian independence.
- Steve Jobs stood for cool, sleek, innovative products.
- Martin Luther King stood for racial and economic equality.
- Malala Yousafzai stands for education for girls.

Your stand as a leader does not have to be as dramatic as these examples. But, whether your goal is large or small, you need to stand for something that is not going to happen automatically.

Your stand needs to be authentically you. In *Authentic Leadership*, Bill George suggests, "The one essential quality a leader must have is to be your own person, authentic in every regard." It can be a relief not to have to be some stereotype of what you believe a good leader should be.

We are quick to criticise our political leaders when they abandon their declared stand in the desperate rush to win votes. We should be just as outraged by corporate leaders who breach their promise to uphold ethical or legal agreements so they can get their company share price up.

In a stand, you declare a future that is important.

Have you ever worked with a leader who did not stand for anything? These types of leaders can be blown around like tumbleweeds, influenced by whoever spoke to them last. Their decisions are often based on political expediency.

This is frustrating and saps the life out of any business, because it is all about survival.

A leader who stands for a future that is not predictable, a future that is not going to happen automatically, breathes life into the organisation.

When you stand for a new future you will of course encounter resistance. Life is drifting along on a certain predictable trajectory, and when you take it in an entirely different direction there will be doubters. It may be that they cannot see how the future you are standing for can be attained.

John F. Kennedy stood for a future in his inauguration speech in 1961. "All this will not be finished in the first 100 days," he said. "Nor will it be finished in the first 1,000 days, nor in the life of this Administration, nor even perhaps in our lifetime on this planet. But let us begin."

That is how you begin to change the game. Dean Phelan took a stand to create a new model of a church when he took over as CEO of Churches of Christ in Queensland. His leadership team created a new future that was about bringing the light of Christ into communities. They integrated the church and community services around their stand.

Following are some examples of stands my own clients have made:

"I am committed to improving the gender diversity of the technology sector."

"I stand for being an authentic leader."

"I promise to be open to other people's contributions."

"I stand for serving by not solving others' problems."

"I support leaders to be as great as they can be."

"I stand for making a difference in the world."

"I stand for living the values we espouse and invite others to call me on it if they see me not doing so."

Your stand will draw people to you. Leadership is essentially about getting results through people, so let's now focus on collaboration.

Collaborate to multiply results

Game-changing leaders collaborate to multiply results. They have a collaborative style, sharing information, insights and learnings. They have clear agendas and wide networks to achieve their results. Their networks extend beyond their own backyard — that is, beyond their own business, industry and profession.

In his book, *What Leaders Really Do*, John Kotter points to a contradiction in leadership theory. Until his research was published it had been assumed that leaders generally follow a traditional military model of leadership, which was to plan, lead, organise and develop. But Kotter found that in fact most successful leaders were not doing that stuff.

More often they were found to be absorbed in apparently inconsequential conversations with people by the watercooler, discussing family matters and shared interests. What Kotter found was that the key to their success was the quality of the relationships they had. And their wide networks enabled them to achieve their ambitious goals.

Kotter is also distinguishing between leadership and management. The job of the manager is to operate and organise and keep things going. This is important work of course, but the other piece of the puzzle is leadership and leading change. It's about changing the game.

The game-changing leader needs to collaborate with a much wider range of stakeholders than someone in a managerial role. A game-changing leader needs to be able to bring people along with them. They need to influence their team, their key stakeholders and even people who are in a position to block their game-changing vision.

So how do you develop a collaborative leadership style? One of the key questions to consider is whether you are a broadcaster or a listener. Leaders with the capacity to really listen to their stakeholders and to inspire their stakeholders' commitment will be more successful.

In her book, *Quiet: The Power of Introverts in a World That Can't Stop Talking,* Susan Cain describes an experiment that compared introvert and extrovert leaders. When set a task of folding a stack of t-shirts, it was found that introvert leaders were more effective because they were more willing to listen to a team member who had been secretly tipped off on a fast way to fold them. Extrovert leaders, on the other hand, did not listen to the team member's advice so missed out on the shortcut.

In Stephen Covey's bestseller, *7 Habits of Highly Successful People*, habit number 5 is "Seek first to understand, then to be understood." Leaders need to be able to balance speaking and listening so they inspire and empower those around them. Covey's key take-out message is to *listen first*.

Game-changing leaders focus on what will forward the conversation. They don't get derailed by conversations that will take the game off course.

How often have you been in a meeting in which things are moving along quite nicely — until suddenly someone says something that completely derails the conversation? For the game-changing leader this is akin to a pilot changing the flight path in mid-flight.

To keep on track, the game-changing leader needs to focus constantly on the end game. They are then able to distinguish between conversations that will divert them from their objectives and conversations that will forward these objectives.

They establish ground rules within their own team about conversations that forward the action. For example, they ask their team members to assess each contribution they consider making in meetings. Will it forward the action? If not, then perhaps they should reconsider raising it. If, for example, someone has already said what you were going to say, then there is no need to repeat it for the sake of hearing your own voice.

If you are to collaborate with others successfully, your mindset is all important.

It's not what you see, it's how you see it

An important part of your personal brand is the mindset you adopt. We all view the world differently, so it's important to examine and choose how we view people and situations.

During the global financial crisis, I read a lot about the gloom and doom the world faced. Based on the news reports, it appeared we were all going down the toilet. But I wanted to know what leaders were thinking about the situation we faced. Accepting the situation at face value, but doing nothing about it, did not seem like leadership to me.

I was heartened to find in the discussions I had with business leaders that their views of the situation were often quite different from how the media were reporting it. Many of them viewed the global financial crisis as an opportunity to reduce costs in areas where they now had a legitimate reason to do so. They were also spotting opportunities to buy other businesses or sell off unprofitable parts of their business. Their conclusion was that there were some great opportunities in adversity.

This story illustrates an important point about how game-changing leaders view the world. The idea of how you view the world as a leader is examined in Steve Zaffron and Dave Logan's book, *The Three Laws of Performance.*

Their first law is that our performance correlates with how we view the world. For example, if during the GFC you were viewing the world only with foreboding, then your performance was likely to correlate with that view. If, on the other hand, you were one of the leaders who viewed it as a period of opportunity, then your performance correlated with that view.

As leaders, we have a choice of how we view the world. There is no single objective view. Take a simple example of a rainy day. When you talk to people about rain, many will enthuse about how good it is for the garden, but others will bemoan the fact that it coincides with their day off! The same situation, but two different views. This seems blindingly obvious to us, but in a more complex example, such as disagreement over a new business strategy, people will argue to the death that their view is the *only right* one.

Clearly we need to pay attention to our own world view, but just as critically, if we are to influence others we need to be aware of their views before we get too far down the track with our new business strategy. It is important to understand how people around us view the situations and challenges they face. By discovering how our team or stakeholders currently view the world, we can understand how their performance will correlate to that view.

The model in figure 8 illustrates the point. You will see that below the line the team is just reacting to what is coming at them. Above the line, they are making things happen. *Where do you think your team is now and where do you want them to be?*

Turbo Team

PERFORMANCE	FUTURE	RESULTS

CREATING

Game-changing	Game-changing	Game-changing
Elite	Inspiring	Exceptional
Superior	Predictable	Acceptable

REACTING

Mediocre	Limited	Flat
Struggling	Stuck	Minimal
Destructive	Demise	Negative

Figure 8: Team diagnostic

Have you ever noticed that a change initiative sometimes gets stuck and goes nowhere? It was a great idea and everyone said they were on board, but when push came to shove it didn't seem to work out. Mostly the reason is that we have not paid attention to how people currently view the world, and we have tried to go forward before realigning on the team's views.

Let's say your team is an IT department. They think of themselves as a backroom order taker and believe the clients don't really understand them. Their performance will correlate with that view of the world, and there is a predictable future that goes with it. Unless they confront that imagined future and decide that's not really what they are committed to, then all the change management and agile methodologies and enhanced governance will make little difference.

If the group decides they don't really want that predicted future, then there is an opportunity to design a new one. It could be that they say the future they are creating is as a strategic advisor to the business. There will then be conversations to end and conversations to start.

For example, a conversation to end could be, "The clients don't know what they're talking about." A conversation to start could be, "We listen to the clients and seek to understand their strategic challenges."

There will also be individual leadership conversations to end and start. Every time the game expands we need to reinforce it with a new level of leadership.

An example of a leadership conversation to end at an individual level could be, "I don't have all the answers." A leadership conversation to start could be, "I am all about providing value to clients."

In her book, *Mindset*, Stanford psychologist Carol Dweck distinguishes between two types of mindset — the fixed mindset, which avoids challenges; and the growth mindset, which embraces challenges. She proposes that leaders with a growth mindset are more inclined to develop other great leaders around them. Leaders with a fixed mindset, on the other hand, will be more likely to make it all about them and their personal ego.

Game-changing leaders with a growth mindset are continually seeking opportunities to forward their game.

Do you have a growth mindset?

Industry incumbents are rarely happy when they are disrupted. In the late 1940s, when the new television technology was being explored in Australia, R.G. Casey, a minister in the Menzies government at the time, opposed it. He expressed a view held by the incumbent radio stations when he said, "We should not add to our already overcrowded market for public entertainment in Australia."

More entrepreneurial minds saw the opportunity of the new technology. Australian television was officially launched in 1956.

There is nothing new under the sun, it seems. With recent news of Amazon's impending launch in Australia, Harvey Norman boss Gerry Harvey dismissed them as "parasites" and said the retailer should be barred from entering Australia. But for many entrepreneurs who own their own brands and are looking for a new way to access bigger markets, the arrival of the $570 billion company represents a game-changing opportunity.

The rapidly changing marketplace will continue to demand game-changing leadership. Global research by IMD suggests that roughly four of today's top 10 incumbents in each industry will be displaced by digital disruption in the next few years.

The leadership mindset is all-important in these disruptive times. In Mindset, Dweck argues that "the view you adopt for yourself profoundly affects the way you lead your life". Her research has demonstrated that those with a fixed mindset see their qualities are carved in stone. As a result, they are more likely to avoid challenges.

Those with a growth mindset, on the other hand, believe we can build on our basic qualities through our ongoing efforts. They are more likely to thrive on challenges and to learn from failures. Game-changing leaders have a growth mindset. They are able to capture opportunities in the face of adversity.

Whether it is building on a strength their organisation already has or seizing an opportunity as it arises, game-changing leaders add value through their growth mindset.

Where could you adopt a growth mindset and create new opportunities to change the game?

Now let's look at the type of communication that game-changing leaders employ to move things forward.

Requests and promises

Have you noticed there's a type of communication that promotes action and forward movement, and there's a type of communication that seems to block it, just talking about things and where nothing seems to happen? One of the essential qualities of a game-changing leader is the ability to have committed conversations that make things happen.

When Graham arrived on the scene in his new job, he inherited a team that seemed to be running frantically from one challenge to the next. He had some ideas of his own, but he decided he would first ask members of his direct report team to recommend possible improvements, particularly regarding customer service. He found, though, that his expectation that he would get something back from them within a few days was constantly thwarted by excuses that this or that emergency had intervened, or they were waiting on someone else for some information. There was a litany of excuses and not much action.

Graham started having committed conversations. He would make a defined request of someone. A request needs a specific "what" by a specific "when". For example, "David, could you complete that report for me about customer improvements by 5.00 p.m. Wednesday?" The person on the other end of the request now had three options. They could accept his request. Or they could make a counter-offer — for example, "I can't do it by 5.00 p.m. Wednesday, but I could manage it by 12.00 p.m. Thursday. Is that okay?" The third option they had was to decline the request.

Once Graham had established that they had accepted or counter-offered, he generally had a promise from the individual that he could record and track, and therefore some accountability. A couple of days before the due date he could get in touch with the person to check whether they were on track. This gave them the opportunity to reaffirm their commitment or request more clarity on what should be included in the report. There was now no room for failure to make the deadline. If that did happen, Graham was in a position to say that was unacceptable and they should keep going until they produced the report.

Graham found that there was now a lot less extraneous conversation around excuses and explanations, most of which was not relevant. In team meetings or discussions with individuals, he now made sure that he did not walk away without a commitment to *what by when*.

We see this in our personal lives too. No doubt you have friends you can absolutely count on. You know, the ones you invite for dinner at 7.00 p.m. on Saturday and there they are, on the dot. But we all have the other types of friends who may come up with a last-minute excuse or arrive half an hour late with some long-winded story. It's just so much more refreshing to be around people who do what they say they'll do.

It's the same in the workplace. So much meeting time is wasted on communication that does not forward action. Conversations about who is to blame, excuses, explanations, stories. This simple process of introducing requests and promises makes life much more rewarding and, more importantly, forwards the action.

As game-changing leaders, we're interested in how to make things happen that were not going to happen by themselves. This means making big commitments. So, all the subsidiary commitments, all the small promises and requests along the way, add up to ensure the big commitment is accomplished. People so readily step over the small commitments (such as getting that report done by Wednesday 5.00 pm) because in themselves they don't really matter that much, but in the larger scheme of things they do matter, if we're to deliver on our promise to change the game.

One way to think about building muscle in making requests of those around you is to think of them as leadership opportunities. No doubt you have been on the receiving end of requests, or perhaps even demands, of you that had you step up. Most of us have had the experience of someone believing in us, perhaps even more than we believed in ourselves at the time. They said, "I want you to take on this big project or this new role," and you may have thought privately or even said aloud, "I don't know if I'm up to this." But they wouldn't have it. "No, no," they said, "you'll be fine." And sure enough, you dug deep and found something hidden that you didn't know you had to deliver on the promise you took on. They gave you an opportunity to expand on your leadership when they made the request of you, knowing you could do it.

All your requests do not have to be huge leadership opportunities, but by making more and more requests of people around you every day, you will build your capacity to cause other leaders to step up. Requests do not need to be in only one direction either. They may not always be aimed downward to members of your team. They could be directed upward to people in management above you, or sideways to peers, or outwards to vendors and suppliers.

For example, a request to a manager above you could be, "Would you come to our team meeting on Monday morning and talk about the new strategy for the business?" It is an opportunity for that leader to demonstrate his or her leadership. A request to one of your peers might be, "Please send me the paper on customer satisfaction by 5.00 p.m. Tuesday," which gives them an opportunity to demonstrate their leadership on a topic they are passionate about. A request outward to one of your strategic suppliers, such as, "Please send me the data on service levels by 6.00 p.m. tomorrow," gives them the opportunity to demonstrate their leadership.

It could, of course, be something like, "Please take on this big project that is off the rails and get it back on track by 31 March," which might provide one of your team members with a big leadership opportunity. But the point here is that not all requests need to be big or demanding.

As a game-changing leader, if you are making more and more requests and eliciting promises for committed action by others, then you will need to expand your system for capturing the promises of what will be done by when. What I mean here is a system that tracks your projects, tasks, meetings and, importantly, the promises that other people make to you. There is no single way of doing this, and I do not want to be prescriptive about what method to use. I have found that leaders need to use a system that works well for them. There are plenty of good books and applications that will help you to manage your time and commitments. The important point is to have some way of recording the requests you make and the promises others make to you. Trying to carry it all in your head is a big mistake.

The main object of recording your requests and promises is to encourage accountability. People will pretty quickly notice if, when a due date arrives and they fail to deliver, you don't notice and there are no consequences. We're all the same, with busy lives and plenty to do, our days quickly fill up without our even trying. It takes real effort to prioritise our promises and deliver on them in the way we said we would.

If you have big expectations of committed action from others, you had better make sure you are walking the talk. That is, that you are, first of all, comfortable making promises to others, including to your peers, to management or to your own your team members when they ask you for something. Your promises need to be recorded in your system somehow, and for the sake of your own personal integrity, you need to make sure you deliver on those promises.

Of course, there will be times when it's not going to be possible to deliver on a promise made. But if this is handled honourably, then it too can forward the action. The moment you know you are not going to be able to deliver on what you promised, get in touch, let them know and renegotiate the agreement. Train those around you to act with a similar level of integrity regarding their promises to you. The moment they know it's not going to be possible to meet their commitment, they need to communicate this to you.

Leadership is about causing other leaders to step up. Did someone cause you to step up your leadership? It is time to pay it forward.

Pay it forward

Dave was a young gun, quick on the uptake and eager to make his mark. There was an exciting energy about him that you could see in his eyes.

His CEO, Bruce, who could see his huge potential, asked him to take on a big new area of accountability that was way outside Dave's comfort zone. At first Dave doubted himself, and said so. He did not want to let his boss down. But Bruce was having none of it — he continued to believe in him.

Sure enough, his faith was well placed. Dave produced outstanding results, tapping into unexpected leadership capabilities. His career took off. And he is happy to attribute his success to the faith that Bruce placed in him. Dave is paying it forward now, giving others the opportunity to step up their leadership.

Why pay it forward? You are only as good as the team you have around you. Back in the day, you built a reputation as a prodigious doer. If necessary you would work day and night to get the job done. But as a leader you soon realise you are going to burn out trying to do everything yourself.

Creating a team of high-performing leaders around you also frees you up to provide the game-changing leadership your stakeholders expect. In my observation, it can accelerate your leadership potential at twice the rate.

One way to create high-performing leaders around you is to challenge them with a stretch objective. If you believe they have what it takes, then you can be confident that they will expand their leadership capability.

Paying it forward is not entirely an altruistic idea. In his book, *Give and Take: Why Helping Others Drives Our Success*, Adam Grant distinguishes between the givers, the takers and the matchers. Grant's research shows that givers end up ahead in the long run.

Do you believe in someone more than they believe in themselves? Maybe you also appreciate the people in your life who have believed in you. A little appreciation can go a long way.

A little appreciation goes a long way

Leaders are only as effective as the team they surround themselves with. That means choosing those people wisely. If you have a great team, the next challenge is getting them to stick around. Appreciation can play a bigger part in retaining good people than we realise.

Tony knew he was fortunate to have a great leadership team. He gave each one of his direct reports his heartfelt appreciation at the end of their strategy session. He recognised them not only for their valuable achievements but also for their unique leadership qualities. He acknowledged one leader for the difference her can-do attitude made. He highlighted how another leader had the ability to keep going in the face of disagreement. For another, he emphasised the courage it took for her to step outside her comfort zone into a big new role.

It made a huge difference to each team member to be acknowledged for the difference they made. Tony had created a new future for every one of them. A future that challenged them to be game-changing leaders. And they were only too happy to pay forward the appreciation to their respective teams. The simple practice of appreciation helped create a culture where people felt valued and wanted to stick around.

People tend to underestimate the benefits of appreciation, which is why it is in such short supply in the workplace. In one US survey, 81 per cent of respondents said they'd be willing to work harder for an appreciative boss; 70 per cent said they'd feel better about themselves and their efforts if their boss thanked them more regularly. And yet just 10 per cent of survey respondents said they themselves regularly showed their colleagues gratitude.

"A sense of appreciation is the single most sustainable motivator at work," Adam Grant argues; "your raise in pay feels like your just due, your bonus gets spent, your new title doesn't sound so important once you have it. But the sense that other people appreciate what you do sticks with you."

Who could you appreciate more?

SIX

Performance: Commit to achieving stretch results

Leaders at the performance stage on the influence curve (figure 9) make big *commitments* and elicit big commitments from those around them.

A characteristic of game-changing leaders is their commitment to achieving stretch results. They are prepared to move outside their comfort zone to achieve their objectives. A point I make often throughout this book is that making big commitments can be a key to unlocking your game-changing leadership capability. When you make a stretch commitment, you need to find a new level of leadership to deliver on your promise. Most, if not all, stretch commitments involve getting results through key stakeholders.

If you only ever make predictable commitments on things you already know you can accomplish, then you will just get more of the same. Game-changing leadership, making big commitments and eliciting big commitments from those around you, enables you to accelerate your leadership potential up to four times.

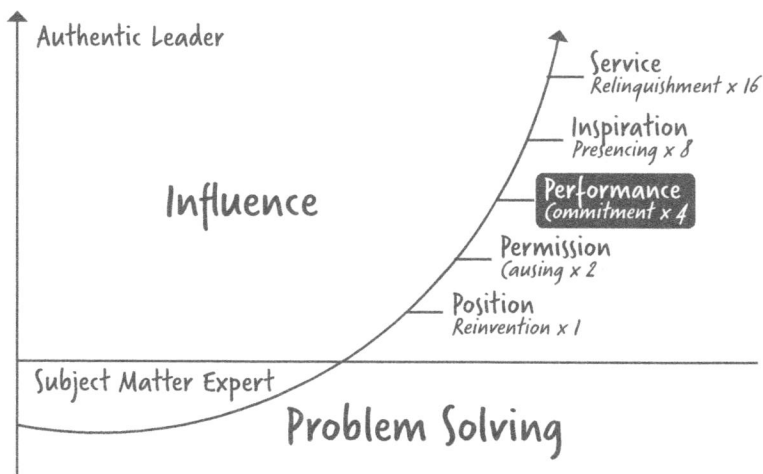

Figure 9: Performance stage on the influence curve

A BIG game is a good game!

The project was off the rails. Major delays and cost overruns were frustrating the project sponsor. Two successive project leaders had already been fired and morale in the delivery team was at an all-time low. Users were disenchanted and the board was getting nervous. Colin was parachuted in with the mission to turn things around.

Colin knew that leadership is a team sport, so the first thing he did was allow the team to vent their frustrations. He then painted a picture of the predictable future if nothing changed. His people reaffirmed that they wanted to be on a winning team. They aligned with him on a new commitment to deliver a successful outcome within six months. That was a stretch commitment. Most stakeholders had accepted that it could take twelve months or more to sort out, if it succeeded at all.

At the time they made the stretch commitment, Colin and the team had little evidence that it was achievable. But having made their pledge, they now needed to see what it would take to deliver on their promise. Colin knew he had to take his leadership to a new level. Critically, he needed to reinvent his strength as a great problem solver. His problem now was how to get the best from his team.

As it turned out, the team surprised themselves and everyone around them by successfully delivering the project. Colin built his personal brand as a can-do guy and is now in demand as a game-changing leader.

Predictable commitments, by definition, will only get you more of what you already have. Game-changing leaders make stretch commitments and are able to elicit big commitments from those around them.

Making big commitments is not an outlandish idea. We have all taken on stretch commitments, whether it was taking on a big new role or becoming a parent. Whatever the case, the commitment is the key, not whether we have the necessary knowledge or skills. We commit, and in the process of delivering on our commitment we discover new resources in ourselves.

It is the nature of a big commitment that it takes us outside our comfort zone. It's all relative, of course. If you are a distance runner, a five-kilometre jog would be child's play, but with my current level of aerobic fitness the idea seems almost unattainable. In my experience, though, it is only in the realm outside our comfort zone that unexpected and surprising results will occur. You need to create a new "game" with a specific and measurable result. Using a sporting analogy, the team members are playing a game they enjoy, giving it everything they have got to achieve a win.

We have all experienced that moment of simultaneous terror and excitement when the full impact of the commitment we have made sinks in. Every parent knows that feeling! People who have transferred to another country or have taken on a big new role that stretches them have also experienced it. If we truly commit, something kicks in that allows us to expand our capacity beyond our and others' expectations.

Committing to something that is important to us is one part of the equation; inspiration is another (figure 10).

If either inspiration or commitment is missing in some area of life that is important to you, then you might consider creating a comfort zone challenge — a BIG game, to propel you into action. Challenge yourself to create something over the next three to six months that is both scary and exciting, committing yourself to the project by sharing your plans with the people around you. You will be surprised by the results you can achieve. If you play flat out, you won't know yourself at the end of it.

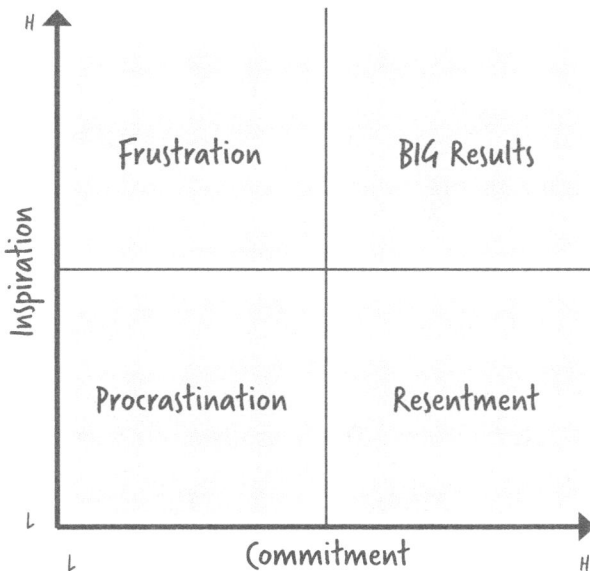

Figure 10: Inspiration + commitment = BIG results

It is this ability to make and achieve stretch commitments that changes the game. Zenger Folkman's research based on 360-degree evaluations of 20,000 individuals suggests that "establishing stretch goals" is one of the 16 competencies of extraordinary leaders. It is a key component of what distinguishes extraordinary leaders from good leaders.

Once you make a stretch commitment you will need to be interested in getting support from people around you to achieve it. We need to shift our focus from ourselves and onto the stakeholders we are trying to influence. When we start to look at the problem through their eyes and can articulate how our stretch objective will help solve a fundamental problem for them, we become truly connected.

I don't doubt that you are a committed person. Clearly you are, or you would not be reading this book. What I am talking about here is the ability to make commitments that you think right now are beyond your capacity.

Yes, that sounds big and scary, but you have probably already done it many times in your work and personal life.

People who have moved countries, for example, take on a big commitment. There is usually no roadmap or instruction book on what to do when you arrive in a new country. But once you have committed to moving you just work things out inside your commitment.

Parents also understand this idea. I regularly ask parents whether they felt they had the training or skills they needed at the time they started their family? Did they think they were ready to be parents? I have yet to hear one person say yes. The point here is that it's not whether you have the knowledge or skills or training; what's important is your commitment. It's your determination as a leader to make stretch commitments and your ability to elicit commitments from the people around you that enable you to change the game.

Imagine that a project leader adds up all the inputs for the project and calculates that it will need two years to complete. But you know you don't have two years, so you propose that they go back and recut the project plan in order to deliver it in six months. The idea is to *commit first*, then work out how to deliver on that commitment, not the other way around.

Often, as soon as you take on a bigger game, what comes up is, "Do I really have what it takes to deliver on this commitment?" To succeed you may need to give up your limiting points of view about yourself and others.

Can you subtract as well as add?

Peter's boss had lost the plot and the board were moving to replace him. The business was not performing well and staff morale was low. Peter and the rest of the leadership team had lost focus. Everyone was waiting for someone else to do something.

Peter took on the responsibility of challenging the leadership team to turn things around while they searched for a new CEO.

It was a personal decision. He had not been given any authority, but people responded well to his leadership and got back into action rather than simply watching the train wreck that was happening around them. Peter worked with his boss to help him make a dignified exit. He handled the arrival of the new CEO with integrity. His willingness to take leadership responsibility during this difficult time was noted by the board.

What people did not see was that Peter had to give up his view that he did not have what it takes to be the one to provide much-needed leadership at this important time. He also changed his view on how others were responding to this difficult situation. Importantly, he surrendered his concern that his peers would think he was getting too big for his boots by taking responsibility for leading the business.

Giving things up is an aspect of leadership that is not often talked about. We are constantly bombarded by the latest list of leadership skills to add to our toolkit in order to be effective leaders. Of course, there is nothing wrong with adding to our repertoire. But are there also things we need to subtract? Like that insidious internal conversation of self-doubt that keeps us playing a safe, small game.

Jack Zenger, CEO of the leadership development firm Zenger Folkman, submits that "a person's demonstrated willingness to behave responsibly" is one of the major reasons why one person is selected for promotion while others with equal skills, education and experience are passed over. More than the position the individual occupies, he argues, it is their attitude to responsibility that is critical. Such an attitude places the goals of the organisation higher than individual or even team goals.

To take on greater responsibility for achieving the goals of the organisation, you may need to give up your limiting points of view about yourself and others.

What could you give up that would allow you to take greater responsibility?

Of course, it does not stop there. To build a personal brand as a game-changing leader, you need to act with integrity.

Why integrity matters

In 2010, BP was responsible for one of the world's worst environmental disasters when the Deepwater Horizon oil rig in the Gulf of Mexico exploded, killing 11 workers and releasing 3.19 million barrels of crude oil into the ocean. In one single event, the company destroyed all the good will they had built up since launching their US$200 million 'Beyond Petroleum' brand campaign in 2000 with its green, clean, environmentally conscious image.

The total pre-tax charge for the spill was US$53.8 billion and in 2013, 43 per cent of Americans still had an unfavourable view of BP. Their brand has taken a hammering from which they may never recover. Their integrity is in question because their actions have been judged to be at odds with the brand values they espouse.

As leaders, we spend considerable time and effort building our personal brand, much as a company builds its brand. Our stakeholders have expectations and perceptions of us, just as they do of the businesses they deal with. And like a business brand, integrity is the critical piece in our personal brand.

It would be easy to succumb to the anecdotal evidence of the current "post-truth" era that honesty and integrity no longer matter. However, the data about what people are looking for in leaders shows a different picture. Gallup asked more than 10,000 followers around the world exactly why they followed the most important leader in their life. At the top of the list was trust, which they also equate with honesty, integrity and respect.

Of course, most of us are convinced we are honest and always act with integrity. But we are judged by our actions rather than our intentions. Our actions need to be consistent with our personal brand as game-changing leaders. Otherwise, like BP, our brand will be judged as mere rhetoric and is likely to be irreparably damaged.

Good brands respond to their customers' perceptions. You can gain valuable insights from canvassing your stakeholders' views of the integrity of your personal brand:

- Do I do what I promise?
- Are my actions consistent with what I say I stand for?

If you are building your personal brand, then you also need the confidence that comes from knowing your value.

Are you confident of your value?

As the only woman on the executive leadership team at the strategic offsite, Heather was reluctant to risk speaking up. She asked the facilitator to present on her area of accountability rather than doing it herself. It was a decision she later deeply regretted. She was sick and tired of holding herself back. She wanted to build her confidence and break out of the protective bubble she had created for herself.

Heather decided to take on a stretch objective to formulate a restructure of the business and present it to the executive leadership team. She recognised that her fear of being seen as an impostor was limiting her. She decided enough was enough; it was time for her to burst out of her protective bubble. Once she made the commitment to break out of her comfort zone, her mindset shifted. Looking back at her past career experience, she began to see evidence of, in her words, "a woman of substance".

She was relieved that she did not need to build her confidence through swagger, aggressive body language or other inauthentic confidence-building strategies that some of her colleagues employed. Her confidence came from knowing her value. And Heather realised that her collaborative strength was just what the siloed business needed. Her mindset shift enabled her to move her focus away from her perceived shortcomings to her stakeholders' problems and the value that she could offer them.

The executive leadership team were delighted with her recommendations. Her views became highly sought after. Now when she spoke at the leadership table people listened. More importantly, Heather saw herself making the difference she had always wanted to make.

In an HBR article, Tony Schwartz suggests, "Great leaders don't feel the need to be right, or to be perfect, because they've learned to value themselves in spite of shortcomings they freely acknowledge. In turn, they bring this generous spirit to those they lead."

Are you confident in your value?

Game-changing leaders use their value to create opportunities to forward their objectives. Their opportunity mindset is like that of an entrepreneur.

Create opportunities to change the game

Frances's keynote address at the CIO conference was a big hit. The audience could all relate to her experience of IT systems being considered too late in mergers, acquisitions or reorganisations. She had a depth of understanding on the topic and recommendations for success that had come from gathering market intelligence on the topic. For them she exemplified the strategic value that CIOs can provide.

A few months earlier she had turned a problem into an opportunity. She was the CIO for a mid-sized company that had neglected to involve her IT department at an early stage of a proposed acquisition. The result was that the systems did not integrate and both organisations were unhappy. Spurred on by her passion to find a better solution, she interviewed people in the market to see what she could learn from their war stories, mistakes and successes when integrating disparate systems.

She saw the opportunity to turn her findings into a white paper followed by personal briefings for those who shared her frustration and were hungry for a best practice template. She put her own recommendations into practice and became known as the go-to person on the topic. She subsequently seized the opportunity to leverage her paper with a keynote address at the CIO conference.

Her widening network of supporters did a great job of advocating for her as a leader who could shake things up. A job offer resulted, and in the process, she transitioned from IT to general management with a go-ahead company. She was also offered other opportunities to pursue her passion for attracting more girls and women into IT. She continues to create opportunities for herself and others around her.

Game-changing leaders like Frances have an opportunity mindset. They seek out and create opportunities to forward their objectives. They may not be running a start-up, but their opportunity mindset is like that of an entrepreneur. They have a clarity of purpose that enables them to create and recognise opportunities. Frances turned the initial problem into an opportunity, which led to a series of further opportunities.

This style of leadership is outlined in the book, *The New Entrepreneurial Leader*, based on research by the authors from Babson College. "Entrepreneurial leaders refuse to cynically or lethargically resign themselves to the problems of the world," they argue. "Rather, through a combination of self-reflection, analysis, resourcefulness, and creative thinking and action, they find ways to inspire and lead others to tackle seemingly intractable problems." The Babson authors found that entrepreneurial leaders shape opportunities within the context of who they are, what they know and who they know.

What opportunities could you create to change the game?

If it is a big game, it will stretch you in new ways and it will not always go your way. Practices for dealing with the inevitable breakdowns are part of the toolkit of game-changing leaders.

It doesn't always go your way

Rock singer Patti Smith broke down in the middle of her performance at the Nobel Prize ceremony in Stockholm in 2016. She was overcome with nervousness when singing in front of a large, distinguished audience that included the King and Queen of Sweden and many Nobel laureates.

Standing in for her childhood hero Bob Dylan, who was being honoured with the Nobel Prize in Literature, she had chosen to sing his "A Hard Rain's a-Gonna Fall". When the words of the second verse did not come, she stopped and tearfully apologised. The audience applauded her and encouraged her to go on. Many were deeply moved by her heartfelt performance. Some would later tell her that it felt like a metaphor for their own struggles.

Leadership is a bit like a public performance. No matter how well prepared you are, it won't always go your way. By definition, if you are a game-changing leader, you will encounter obstacles and resistance. The question is how you deal with these inevitable setbacks?

> **"Anyone can hold the helm**
> **when the sea is calm."**
> – Publilius Syrus –

In a sense, leadership can be pretty easy when everything is going well, when there is not much to do other than to keep the ship on course. It is in the challenging moments that we need to step up our leadership, to dig deep. Warren Bennis and Robert J. Thomas call these transformative crises that shape leaders "crucible experiences", after the vessel used by medieval alchemists when attempting to turn base metals into gold. They argue that challenging experiences help define us as leaders. "The skills required to conquer adversity and emerge stronger and more committed than ever are the same ones that make for extraordinary leaders."

Patti Smith said, "...in the end I had to come to terms with the truer nature of my duty. Why do we commit our work?... It is above all for the entertainment and transformation of the people. It is all for them. The song asked for nothing. The creator of the song asked for nothing. So why should I ask for anything?"

What are the crucible experiences that have defined your leadership?

SEVEN

Inspiration: Inspire others by making the future present

Leaders at the inspiration stage of the influence curve (figure 11) are able to make the future vision so *present* for others that it is clear what action needs to be taken today. They have the ability to articulate a vision and bring others along on the journey so they also own the vision.

Recent research by Culture Amp supports the view that employees want leaders who can "provide a vision that people believe in and are motivated by". When Martin Luther King delivered his "I have a dream" speech, he was able to make his vision for freedom and equality so present that people could see the action they needed to take.

Leaders at this level accelerate their leadership potential up to 8 times.

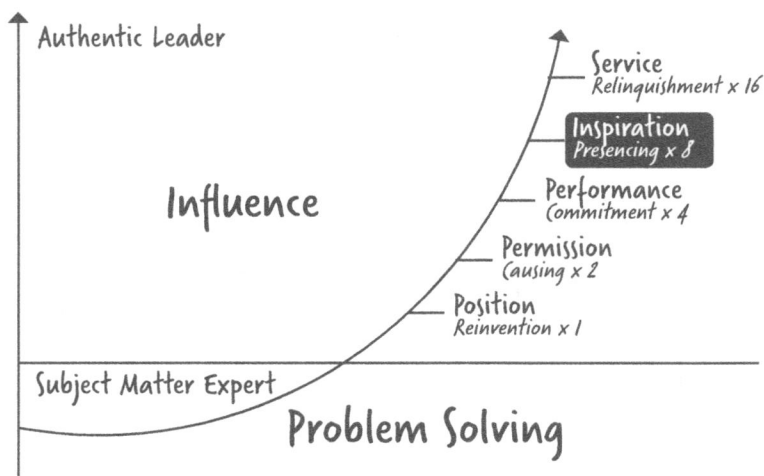

Figure 11: Inspiration stage on the influence curve

Why do you do what you do?

Sipping her coffee at her usual early-morning coffee shop, Ruth told the barista, "You make a fantastic coffee. It's exactly the way I like it." He said, "Oh, I don't just make coffee, I make your day!" He explained that if she gets her coffee just the way she likes it — hot, strong, with no sugar, in a large cup — then her day gets off to a great start. On the other hand, if she begins with a bad cup of coffee, her day would not look nearly so good!

The barista had created a context for his job that was way bigger than making coffee. He was actually a medical student working part time, so an equally valid context for him could have been that he was making coffee while waiting to do his real job in life.

Both contexts would have been accurate. But the context he had created — that his job was about making people's day — was way more inspiring for him and for the customers he served.

For game-changing leaders, context is critical, both for our own inspiration and for our broader team and stakeholders. There is a world of difference between a context of delivering the project on time and on budget and delivering a project that changes the customer experience of your organisation. Similarly, achieving the sales target by the end of the quarter may not be nearly as satisfying a context as finding customers who love our solutions and become our raving fans.

Leaders who create a bigger context, one that requires a new level of leadership, are more likely to change the game. Simon Sinek, in his TED Talk *How Great Leaders Inspire Action*, argues that great leaders inspire action because they "start with why": WHY do we believe what we are doing is important?

What is a context for your current leadership challenge that would inspire you and others?

If you have a powerful context in which to change the game, you will also need to bring your team along with you to deliver the stretch objective.

Inspire the team to multiply results

When Graham took on his new leadership role he initially spent a lot of time discovering how people viewed the viability of the organisation. He asked them what they saw as the predictable future if nothing changed. It seemed obvious to him that the successful parts of the business would be sold off while the groups that were not doing well would steadily decline.

People said that they more or less knew where things were headed but that the organisation would probably limp along for another few years. They had not fully confronted the personal impact of the business's inevitable demise.

Graham stepped out the phases of the predictable future for them. The company's reputation would suffer and talented people would leave, while new talent would not be attracted to work with them. Those who were left would be in survival mode, waiting for the business to be eventually sold. The death by a thousand cuts did not seem like a future that would get them out of bed in the morning.

The leadership team confronted the reality that there could be no satisfaction or fulfilment in drifting along toward extinction. They were galvanised into creating and aligning on a vision for a new future for the organisation. They were also inspired to take the next step and set themselves stretch objectives to achieve it.

Rather than being a vision that had been thrust on them by Graham, this was something they owned. He had helped them shift the way they viewed what was possible for the organisation. Graham knew that he could not transform the organisation himself and that he could multiply his results with an aligned leadership team.

The organisation became a model for transformation in their sector and was soon attracting interest from like-minded organisations.

Aligning a leadership team and unlocking their leadership potential takes finesse. The authors of *The Three Laws of Performance* suggest, "Leaders have a say and give others a say in how situations occur." Graham was happy that he did not always have to be "the sharpest knife in the drawer". He had surrounded himself with good leaders who were willing to grasp the opportunity to create a new future.

How could you align your team on a new future?

Your ability to bring your team along with you also depends on listening to what is important for them. Similarly, to become a trusted adviser to your key stakeholders, game-changing leaders need to be good listeners, not just broadcasters.

Listen and connect to change the game

My 92-year-old father has the ability to connect with others in a way I can only aspire to. Recently I took him to the pathology clinic for blood tests. At reception a sullen nurse, who did not even look up as she asked our business, gestured us to a seat. I was annoyed by her behaviour and concerned that my dad would be on the receiving end of her grumpiness. Much to my surprise, however, when they came out after his tests, they were fast friends. I asked my dad what had happened while they were together that had caused such a transformation. She had looked quite worried to him, so he asked her sympathetically if she was having a bad day, whereupon she had poured out her problems to him. They were short-staffed, she told him and she had been under enormous pressure all day.

My father had listened intently, as he always does, and agreed with her that it must indeed be hard to cope with all she had on her plate. He completely got the nurse's experience. He did not offer any solutions to fix her problems. But my dad's interest in her and his willingness to understand what her world was like completely transformed the situation. They were now on first-name terms and had exchanged details about their families. By the time we left, the nurse was glowing.

Later I reflected on the power of that type of listening. By connecting with people around us in that way, we are halfway to achieving our objective of being a trusted adviser to our key stakeholders.

Stephen R. Covey puts it well in his timeless book, *The 7 Habits of Highly Effective People*. Habit no. 5 is "Seek first to understand, then to be understood". How much time is spent preparing for what we want to say rather than listening to our stakeholders and understanding their problems? My father's example showed how a whole new world opens up if we first invest in understanding the other person's experience.

For the introverts among us, there is also the reassurance of knowing that listening is a powerful leadership attribute.

How could you better listen to understand your key stakeholders?

Now, having spent the time to listen to your stakeholders, what does it take to provide them with an experience of a lifetime?

Do your customers have the experience of a lifetime?

My dad was like a boy again when he recently visited the engine control room on board a cruise ship. He had worked in engine rooms on ships in the Australian Navy in the Second World War and was very excited to be back on board a ship, let alone in the engine control room, for the first time in 71 years. The chief engineer on board our cruise ship generously explained how modern engine rooms powered these floating hotels.

Talk about delighting the customer. My father said it was the experience of a lifetime.

It made me reflect on the idea of customer experience. Many companies have customer experience departments that are interested in understanding our experience of using their products and services. Of course, some of it is mere sloganeering, like Microsoft's professed customer obsession, but I digress!

But what about the internal customer experience? How would your internal clients, key stakeholders and team members rate their experience of working with you? Many of us have worked with a leader who changed the course of our career. Are you being that leader for others?

Interestingly, Temkin Group reports a correlation between employee engagement and success in customer experience. Their research shows that companies that excel at customer experience have one and a half times as many engaged employees as the laggards.

If you regard yourself as a business of one, your internal customer's experience is critical. What does it take to provide people around you with an experience of a lifetime?

Gallup's list of top things that followers seek in their leaders may provide some inspiration:

- **Trust** (other words cited by followers were *honesty, integrity* and *respect*)

- **Compassion** (other words cited by followers were *caring, friendship, happiness* and *love*)

- **Stability** (other words cited by followers were *security, strength, support* and *peace*)

- **Hope** (other words cited by followers were *direction, faith* and *guidance*)

What else could you do to provide an experience of a lifetime for your internal stakeholders, clients and team members?

Game-changing leaders create a new future in collaboration with those around them. They do that through a series of conversations.

Leadership is a conversation

My good friend and colleague, Dean Phelan, retired recently as CEO of Churches of Christ in Queensland. His premature retirement came after he was diagnosed with Acute Myeloid Leukaemia and stepped down for the good of the organisation. He is now well on the road to recovery and continues to inspire us with his positivity in adversity. Reflecting on his leadership serves to inspire the very best in us.

One way of thinking about the leadership he provided is as a series of conversations.

When he took over he discovered a siloed organisation. The traditional Church side of the organisation was dwindling, like most churches around the globe. A separate and growing community services arm was providing important services to the aged, homeless, youth and foster care sectors. The prevailing narrative about the organisation that appeared in annual reports, public statements and internal staff communication was that they were an organisation comprised of seventy churches with an ancillary community support services role.

Dean could see that the story they told needed to be reinvented.

He started a series of conversations about the predictable future for the organisation if nothing changed. Church attendance numbers were steadily declining, with an ageing population not being replaced by young people for whom attending church on Sundays was not relevant. It was likely the community services arm would further separate, with some sectors being sold off. Clearly a single strategy aimed at growing more churches was not viable. If they continued on their current trajectory, then their dissolution was inevitable.

Dean conducted a further series of conversations with his leadership team and community leaders to create a new future. They aligned on a new mission for the organisation to "bring the light of Christ into communities". They reversed the traditional model of individual churches and care businesses separately trying to grow their own numbers and positioned the local community's needs as the main focus. They brought Christian values of service to the community instead of regarding the church building as the only touch point for people.

In the process, they established integrated services by providing affordable housing for the homeless, care for the elderly, care and protection for at-risk children and youth, men's sheds, counselling support and many more services that served the physical, mental, emotional and spiritual needs of individuals and families in each community.

Game-changing leaders like Dean are adept at generating future-based conversations. They paint a picture of a possible future that inspires people to take urgent action.

But to be effective and deliver a game-changing outcome they also need to gain ownership from the team around them. The big game to create a new model for the Church also required Dean's leadership team to expand their own personal leadership conversations. They took ownership of the new mission and continue to carry it forward. Dean would be the first to acknowledge that he could accomplish such game-changing objectives only with the support of his leadership team.

How could you change the conversation and align your team on a bold new future?

I believe that leaders like Dean address two key factors to drive the success of their businesses. The first is to generate conversations that are based in the future: a vision of what is possible for the business. The second success factor is to elicit strong ownership of those future-based conversations from within the organisation, with their people aligning themselves with the vision and strategy. Figure 12 illustrates the game-changing outcome of getting those two ingredients to match. It also indicates the consequences of falling short on one or both of those factors.

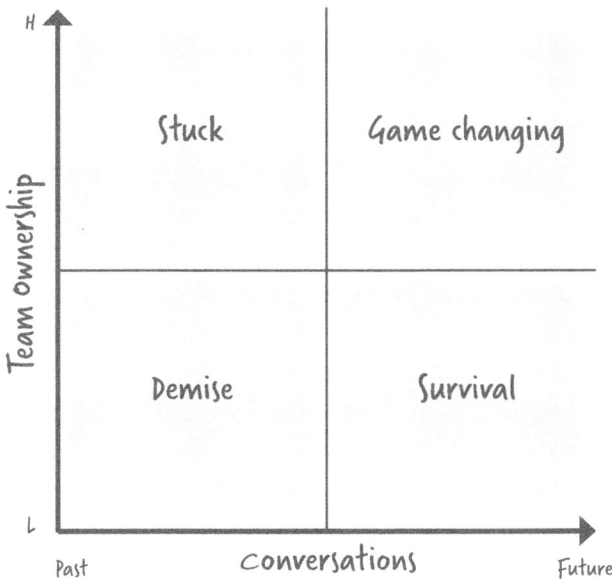

Figure 12: Own the future to change the game

99

Some examples might help clarify these points:

- Let's say you are in the bottom left quadrant — a past-based conversation prevails and there is low ownership of the future. As smartphones burst onto the scene, mobile phone giant Nokia needed to become more innovative. But it appears that at the same time the business was also becoming more bureaucratic, which was stifling innovation. Their past-based conversation and the low organisational ownership of their strategy combined to lead to their failure.

- Perhaps you find your organisation in the top left quadrant — a past-based conversation prevails but in this case, there is high ownership of the strategy. Think Kodak and digital photography as an example of how an organisation strategy of high ownership can still be stuck in a past-based conversation (insisting that film photography was the way to go).

- If you are in the bottom right quadrant, you will at least be talking about a new future, but there is low ownership of it in the organisation. Current examples of print, music and TV illustrate the innovator's dilemma of starting a future-based conversation about the need to change the game, but lacking organisational commitment to a new strategy. The resistance to change from within the organisation is exacerbated when the existing business is still profitable.

- The aspirational quadrant in the top right is where there is a future-based conversation and high ownership of that future. The introduction of the Apple iPhone in 2007 changed the game for mobile phones and consumer computing. At that time, Apple had a powerful future-based conversation about the game-changing nature of the iPhone and strong organisational ownership of the vision. Of course, now that the market has caught up with them they are being pushed to change the game yet again.

What does it take to inspire others to take ownership of a new future? Maybe it is all in the listening.

Executive presence: what is it and how do you get more of it?

Ray was captivated by the conversation he had with a CEO he met at a recent function. Here was an example of a leader with "executive presence", he told me. Intrigued, I asked him to describe the conversation. Ray said the CEO simply asked each person at the table they shared to talk about themselves, their business, the role they played and the challenges they faced, and he *listened* intently to their responses. On stage presenting to a wider audience at the event, he also demonstrated his presence through his understanding of the challenges they faced.

It would be easy for cynics to dismiss the seemingly intangible concept of executive presence, but that would be unwise given how often it is specified in selection criteria for leadership roles. In fact, I regularly meet executives who have received the feedback that they lack executive presence. In some cases, this has stalled their careers, and they are perplexed about what to do about it.

Where do you start if you want to develop more executive presence?

In her book, *All the Leader You Can Be: The Science of Achieving Extraordinary Executive Presence*, Suzanne Bates defines executive presence as "the qualities of a leader that engage, inspire, align, and move people to act". Having thoroughly researched the elusive topic, she offers a model that proposes a systematic way of thinking about executive presence. A key dimension in her model is *character*, which she describes as one of the fundamental qualities that give us a reason to trust a leader.

She breaks down character into five aspects, which were a perfect fit for the qualities of the CEO who had so impressed Ray:

- **authenticity** — he was genuine and transparent
- **integrity** — he appeared to live up to the standards he set
- **concern** — he was genuinely interested in others
- **restraint** — he had a calm, modest disposition
- **humility** — his focus was on others, and he demonstrated a belief that all people have worth.

Rather than being self-absorbed, this CEO was fully "present" in the conversations he had with the people around him. Perhaps executive presence is not such an elusive quality. It is surely a characteristic that differentiates game-changing leaders from the rest.

How can you develop your executive presence to engage, inspire, align and move people to act?

EIGHT

Service: Be of service by relinquishing control

The focus at the service stage of the influence curve (figure 13) is on *relinquishment*. Leaders at this level have become aware that the vision is bigger than them and the focus is on relinquishing control to others. They can confidently relinquish control because they have already coached, supported and empowered others around them to be great leaders.

Relinquishing control enables them to achieve two things. First, they can free themselves up to move on to the next game-changing vision. Second, they can empower others to extend their vision beyond what they originally envisaged.

Leaders at this level accelerate their leadership potential up to 16 times.

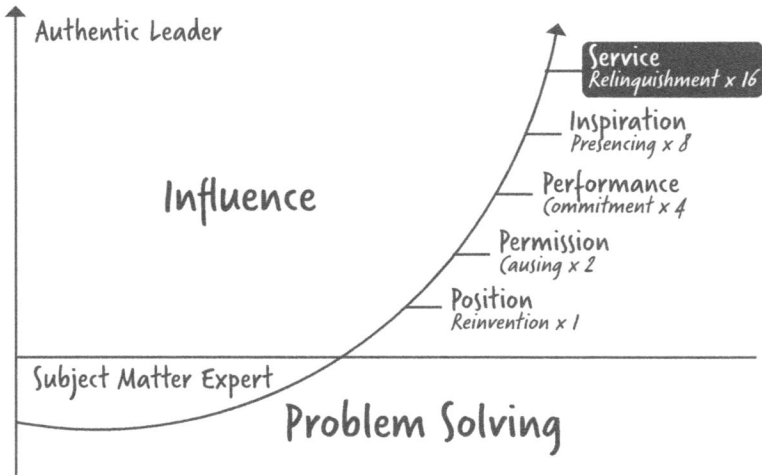

Figure 13: Service stage on the influence curve

Who are your role models?

What organisational leader has the most positive influence in your life? A Gallup poll asked that question of more than 10,000 people in a study of leadership from the follower's perspective. Who would you nominate? Perhaps a leader who influenced your early career, or someone who still inspires you to go the extra mile?

Gerry Moriarty has long been a role model for me and countless others. He will be embarrassed by my acknowledgement. But as he retires from his advisory role with Macquarie Banking Group, I have reflected not just on his significant accomplishments, but on the attributes that make him such a respected and successful leader. What can we learn from leaders like him?

Gerry illustrates the idea that leadership is essentially about getting results through other people. He also exemplifies the point that leadership is about constant adaptation and reinvention. Over the years he has reinvented his career several times. He has carried his inherent problem-solving strength with him from his technical roots in engineering into management and from broadcasting to multimedia to telecommunications, as well as investment banking.

Like many great leaders he is very good at simplifying complex problems. His thinking is uncluttered. He understands that the biggest problem is people. Thinking about how he was able to influence me and so many others to go that extra mile, I noticed three simple but effective practices:

- **He took an interest in you.** He took the time to ask questions about your family, your kids' education, your travel plans, your health and so on. He was genuinely interested in you and valued you as a person.

- **He believed in you.** On many occasions he demonstrated that he believed in me — more than I believed in myself sometimes. In doing so, he challenged me, and many others like me, to keep stepping up our leadership.

- **He said please and thank you.** He would acknowledge that you already had a lot on your plate. He would ask, please will you take on this big new challenge, and he would always make sure to thank you when you delivered the outcome.

It turns out that these attributes are the very qualities that followers are seeking in leaders, according to Gallup's survey.

Gerry's problem-solving strength has enabled him to adapt to new industry sectors and reinvent himself in a successful career that included spearheading Telstra's technology infrastructure, and investment and advisory work at Macquarie.

The important lesson for me from Gerry's example is his continual reinvention and application of his problem-solving and staff motivation strengths. It demonstrates that you can apply your strengths and take them to the next level in new environments. The same strength that got you to where you are now will take you to the next level. Gerry applied his problem-solving ability to the biggest problem of all: how to get the best out of people.

What organisational leader has had the most positive influence in your life?

This leads us toward an understanding that leadership causes culture, not the other way around.

Leadership causes culture, not the other way around

Tony's leadership team confronted the predictable future they could look forward to if they failed to change. Once an important group, they now risked becoming irrelevant. They refused to accept the depressing prospect of gradual demise. Once they decided to challenge their predictable fate, they were able to design a new future. It was a future based on their commitment to make a difference in the lives of their clients. They took on a bigger game to convert their words into action. They identified the conversations and practices they needed to end and to start to support their new future. Now they are stepping up their leadership. Through their actions, they are creating and owning a new culture for their organisation.

Tony recognised that he needed to model what he was seeking from his leadership team. He had seen too many culture change programs fail because of a lack of executive ownership. He did not want to follow examples he had known where a list of values was posted on the wall and all too soon ignored. He knew he would need to step up his own leadership before he could expect his leadership team to do the same. That meant he did not have to pretend to have all the answers. The leadership team valued his authenticity and the opportunity to design the future together.

Tony's story illustrates the point that leadership causes culture not the other way around. Netflix CEO Reed Hastings offers another example of the power of leadership in causing culture. He recently launched a new version of the document Netflix uses to communicate its corporate values to existing and potential employees. The previous version of the statement inspired over 17 million views on SlideShare. Netflix challenges conventional wisdom with its culture statement. Here is an example from the document: "On a dream team, there are no 'brilliant jerks'. The cost to teamwork is just too high."

What is the culture you are creating?

If you create a culture where people run with your ideas, you accelerate your own career objectives.

How to accelerate your career objectives

Don inspired people with a vision of a whole new future for their organisation. One very excited group picked up on his ideas and started to make big things happen. They invited him to come and see the results they were producing. He was blown away by how much further they had expanded on what he had originally envisaged. It was consistent with his objectives, though.

When we spoke later about the visit he was initially disappointed, saying they talked as though it was their concept when it was actually based on his idea. But he had barely expressed this thought when he realised that having the team take ownership of the vision was in fact a very good thing. He did not need the recognition; he had already had plenty of that in his career. The fact that they thought it was their idea meant they would take it beyond where they would have gone if it had been imposed on them. He wanted results, and the team was delivering them.

Once he gave up his desire to be seen as top dog he realised that two things were possible. First, he could move his attention to the next team and the results they could produce to forward his vision. Second, he was no longer the "lid" on the team; they could step up their own level of leadership and produce even bigger results than he had thought possible.

The influence curve is our attempt to codify the stages of influence that leaders go through as they expand their ability to produce results through others. Don was in the service stage of the influence curve, where he was relinquishing control to a capable team.

James Zenger surveyed over 60,000 employees to see which leadership characteristics made leaders "great" in the eyes of their employees. Interestingly, he found that neither a *people* nor a *results* focus alone consistently produced great leadership. Rather, leaders who balanced their focus equally on results and people were seen as great 72 per cent of the time.

Therein lies the opportunity to accelerate your career objectives. Leaders who expand their ability to influence others to produce big results are the game-changers that the market will increasingly seek.

How can you balance your focus on people and results?

Let's see how game-changing leaders further increase the demand for their services through building a personal brand of long-term value.

Jeff Bezos is playing a long-term game. Are you?

Jaws dropped when Amazon recently announced its intention to purchase grocery chain Whole Foods for

US$13.7 billion (AUS$18 billion). What are the leadership lessons from the announcement?

One obvious answer is that no business is immune from disruption. As the lines between technology and business blur, Amazon, a technology business, moves into an adjacent bricks-and-mortar industry. John McDuling, writing in the *Australian Financial Review*, put it this way: "The distinction between tech and business is becoming irrelevant. Amazon is a trendsetter in many ways. So, don't be surprised if more deals like this happen." But what are the leadership lessons from the long-term game that Jeff Bezos is playing? He has presided over a meteoric rise in Amazon's share price over the past two decades. What are the principles that are driving his success? "What we're really focused on," he says, "is thinking long term, putting the customer at the center of our universe and inventing."

Recent research suggests that Bezos is onto something with his long-term thinking. Those companies that operate with a long-term mindset have consistently outperformed their industry peers across almost every financial measure that matters.

Bezos's principles could be applied equally to your own personal leadership as at company level. For example, game-changing leaders are building a personal brand of long-term value. Being customer-centric with your own clients and stakeholders ensures they become your advocates. Continual reinvention of your own leadership goes hand in hand with changing the game.

Are you playing a long-term game with your leadership?

In the long-term game, showing respect is one of the most effective behaviours a leader can demonstrate.

Respect is simple but powerful

Ross gave Gary a big hug when he returned to work after several members of his immediate family were killed in a terrible car accident. Ross did not mind that his hard-bitten executive leadership team members were watching. He knew that it would not be easy for Gary to come back to work after facing such a tragedy. He was genuinely concerned for Gary and his spontaneous hug was an expression of his support for him given what he was going through.

Gary was moved by the simple gesture, and even though this all happened many years ago, he has never forgotten it.

Showing respect for people is a simple aspect of leadership but is also one of the most effective behaviours that a leader can demonstrate. Building trust and respect in the way Ross did is a "soft" skill with a hard business benefit. A 2015 study showed that high-trust companies "are more than 2½ times more likely to be high performing revenue organizations" than low-trust companies. Yet over half (54 per cent) of US employees surveyed claimed they were not regularly shown respect by their leaders. Being too busy for common courtesies is no excuse.

Doug Conant, former CEO of Campbell's Soup, is an example of a leader who treated employees with respect and reaped the business benefit. In his nine years as CEO, he wrote more than 30,000 individualised notes of thanks to his 20,000 employees. In that time, he took the business from near collapse to setting performance records, including outpacing the S&P fivefold.

Conant and Stephen Covey outline three steps to building trust, connecting with people and making them feel valued:

- **Declaring intent** — affirming clearly what people can expect from you as a leader

- **Demonstrating respect** — walking the talk of your declaration

- **Delivering results** — doing the right thing, in the right way, for the right reasons, in the way you said you would.

How can you build trust and respect with the people around you?

Satisfaction and acknowledgement go hand in hand if you are playing a big game. Acknowledging your accomplishments along the way will give you and your team a greater sense of satisfaction and fulfilment.

Are you busy going nowhere?

On the eve of an offsite strategy session with a senior leadership team it became clear that they were more than a little reluctant to attend. Everyone was already stretched to the limit, so the prospect of grappling with a new, bigger strategy was daunting.

We realised that they had never actually been acknowledged for the great job they had done delivering on the current strategy to date. After dinner Terry, the CEO, went around the room and acknowledged the work each member of the leadership team had done in getting the organisation to the significant point they were at now. He chose a few things that each person had contributed to the organisation's overall success. He thanked them for their values, their determination, their contribution to others, their 'can do' approach. He acknowledged the unique contribution each person had made.

This acknowledgement made a huge difference — so much so that the next morning they came to the strategy session eager to take on the next challenge. It was a salutary reminder of the power of acknowledgement and appreciation. Martin Seligman, the doyen of the positive psychology movement, summed it up like this: "Past successes make us feel more confident and optimistic about future attempts."

You will surely have come across busy people who accomplish a lot but never seem to be satisfied or fulfilled. Busy going nowhere, or so it seems to them, they are reluctant to consider a new game-changing strategy because they are already stretched. They tell you there is no time to stop and acknowledge their good work because "we are not done yet".

Satisfaction and acknowledgement are closely linked. If you are playing a big game, you are never done. Nonetheless, acknowledging your accomplishments along the way will give you and your team a greater sense of satisfaction and fulfilment.

It is too easy to be anxious about the gap between what we have accomplished and where we want to be. Focusing only on that gap can rob us of the satisfaction and fulfilment that comes with making meaningful progress.

A good place to start is to acknowledge two or three things you have accomplished today. This practice can be extended to weekly, quarterly and annual milestones.

As Terry found with his team, a little acknowledgement goes a long way.

What are the things you are proud of having accomplished? And who could you acknowledge for their great work?

PART 3

What's Next?

NINE

You are a business of one

Each of us is a business of one, whether we are a business owner or work for an employer. In their book, *Business Model You*, Tim Clark, Alexander Osterwalder and Yves Pigneur make the point that we need a personal business model in much the same way as a company does. Just like any business's, our personal business model needs to be continually reinvented as the environment changes.

A key component of a good business model is the value proposition that the business provides. It solves some problem that the customer faces and is adjusted as the market changes. Similarly, if you think of yourself as a business of one, you will continually refine the value you provide for your customers or stakeholders.

Sandra is a good example of someone who successfully reinvented her value proposition. In the early part of her career, she was known for her ability to get ten things done in the time it would take others to do just one thing. She was highly sought after because she could be counted on to get a difficult job done quickly.

As she moved into leadership, however, she realised that her strength was also her weakness. She would often tell herself, "It's just quicker to do it myself," rather than explain it to her team. But now the scale and complexity of the problems were dramatically greater. Her employer needed her to solve the strategic problems the business faced, not the tactical issues.

She redefined her value proposition from being a prodigious "doer" to being a leader who could "cause" big results through others. To move up the influence curve, she set herself the objective of gaining stakeholder endorsement for a strategy to capture a new market for her company. She aligned her team and was successful in developing and executing a game-changing strategy. Her unique approach was modelled elsewhere in the business.

Sandra is still seen as a reliable results producer, but now she is also known for producing game-changing results. She was recently appointed to a high-level executive role to open up a new market in the Asia-Pacific. The reinvention of her personal business model has given her the satisfaction of making a bigger difference. It has also relieved her from running harder and harder by trying to do everything herself.

Is it time to reinvent your personal business model?

Download a one-page personal business model canvas from Business Model You to help you get started.

How will that help you secure the job of your dreams?

Securing the job of your dreams

How do you secure the job of your dreams — you know, the one where you cannot believe you get paid to do what you do?

When Gary was made redundant from his job, he decided he wanted a global opportunity for his next role. He talked with people in his network about global trends in his area of expertise. Initially he thought the meetings were a waste of time, mainly because no-one was offering him a job. But he persisted with the meetings, knowing he was exchanging valuable intelligence about his market.

A few months after meeting with one firm, they contacted him urgently to say they were putting together a team for a major acquisition in Europe. They did not advertise the job or conduct a search process. They knew he would be perfect for the opportunity and asked him to fly out a few days later.

He worked on the deal, which turned into a job in Europe, where he spent the next two years of his life. He had secured his dream job and the global opportunity he had sought. But it did not end there. His international experience made him even more attractive and he was soon brought back to Australia for a five-year stint. So, seven years of his career turned on a meeting he had initially thought a waste of time.

Figure 14 captures the three-part process that was key to his success. Align what you want on the value you offer and, importantly, on what the market wants — and magic can happen.

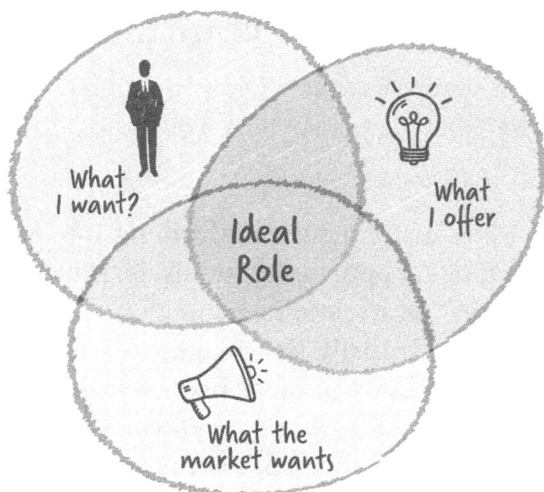

Figure 14: Securing the job of your dreams

The lesson here is that if you gather wide intelligence about what the market wants in your area of expertise you will be well placed to offer your value whether through an advertised position, a search process or a specifically created role, as happened with Gary. That is how you secure the job of your dreams.

What does the market want in your area of expertise?

Of course, game-changing leaders continue to develop their leadership capability and the value they offer.

Exceptional leaders practise self-development

The feedback, from the business unit clients to the CEO, was that they were unhappy with the IT department. Projects were off the rails; day-to-day operations were patchy and there was no confidence that IT could contribute to business strategy. It was only a matter of time before Grant, the CIO, was pushed through the revolving door. Of course, he was equally sure that the clients did not know what they wanted and changed their priorities when it suited them. Plenty of people would have agreed with him. But something had to give.

Grant decided to focus on his leadership behaviour to see if he could shift the needle on client satisfaction.

He had a quick intellect and a great ability to cut through the clutter, but his stakeholders saw him as abrasive. He recognised that his analytical strength was both a blessing and a curse. Sure, he could come up with a quick solution to a problem; on the other hand, he was less successful at bringing his key stakeholders, including his own team, along with him. In fact, he was impatient if they did not keep up.

He dedicated time with his business unit clients to listen to their priorities and understand their market challenges. He instituted regular progress reporting to track the projects they were sponsoring and a client satisfaction survey to capture their perceptions.

The clients responded well to Grant's new approach and started to take ownership of the program of work. His team modelled Grant's behaviour and brought a partnership attitude to their client relationships instead of playing the blame game. Far from being shown the door, Grant is now seen as a valuable member of the executive leadership team and an asset to the business.

Grant's leadership behaviour was critical in transforming the relationship with his clients. In chapter 6, I noted Zenger Folkman's research identifying 16 "differentiating competencies" and the allied behaviours that set highly effective leaders apart. A strength in even one of these competencies will mean you are more likely to be perceived as an outstanding leader in your organisation.

One of the competencies is defined as "Practices self-development". Key behaviours that support this competency are:

- Seeks feedback from others to improve and develop.

- Makes constructive efforts to change and improve based on feedback from others.

- Constantly looks for developmental opportunities.

- Continually develops depth and breadth in key competencies.

- Demonstrates a curiosity toward learning.

- Takes ownership of own development.

- Looks for ways to build challenge into current assignments.

- Learns from both success and failure.

- Models self-development and embraces its value.

What is a key behaviour you could embrace?

Your key behaviours are an integral part of your personal value proposition.

What is the problem that your unique value proposition solves?

What is the problem that people want solved when they buy a milkshake? One study of customers who bought an early-morning milkshake from a fast-food outlet produced an interesting answer. People said that milkshake helped quell their hunger on a long, boring commute.

Understanding the customer's problem makes it easier to meet their needs — in this case by producing a thicker milkshake so it would last longer!

Harvard Business School professor Theodore Levitt famously put it this way: "People don't want to buy a quarter-inch drill. They want a quarter-inch hole!"

Some companies get the point. Hilti is featured in the book, *Value Proposition Design* as an example of a business that realised their value proposition needed to change. Their customers faced the critical problems of delivering projects on time and budget. Lost, damaged or stolen tools only delayed projects. Hilti moved from selling machine tools to embracing a new value proposition: offering leased services, which solved the customer's problem of timeliness.

This is an example of a company value proposition that responded to the actual problems their customers faced. It is equally important to have a responsive personal value proposition as part of your brand. You need to make clear how your value solves a problem for your client or employer.

Why do you need a responsive personal value proposition? According to one survey, four in five Australians leave their job because of limited career opportunities.

Dick Bolles, author of *What Color Is Your Parachute?*, says, "Most job-hunters who fail to find their dream job fail not because they lack information about the job market, but because they lack information about themselves."

Your unique value proposition should help solve a problem for your client or employer. For example, your problem-solving strength could help them avoid a risk they face. Your big-picture strength could help them capture a new opportunity. Your can-do value proposition could support them to execute a strategy their stakeholders love.

Most of us spend very little time thinking about the value we offer, let alone the real problem this solves for our clients and employers.

What is the problem that your unique value proposition solves?

Getting clarity about your unique value proposition not only solves a problem in the market, but also helps you realise your potential.

Are you realising your potential?

My friend Ted Holmes launched his tenth book of poetry at his 95th birthday celebration. He invited his family and friends to return in another five years for his centenary celebration. He is always looking ahead. His latest project is to complete a higher degree focused on the themes he explores in his considerable body of poetry. Ted views his potential as not being limited by his age.

I often try to engage with Ted about his illustrious past. He was a lecturer in accounting at Melbourne University and a pioneer of triple bottom line reporting. He held senior positions in government and industry. He has valuable insights into how humble auditors and accountants transformed themselves into playing strategic leadership roles as Chief Financial Officers and beyond. But he rarely wants to discuss the past. He would rather talk about the future, about his next project.

Ted is my aspirational role model. His future is always bigger than his past. There is the sense about him that he wants to make a big difference and that despite his age he has not yet fully realised his potential.

Robert Steven Kaplan suggests that asking ourselves the question "Am I reaching my potential?" is not the same as asking "How do I rise to the top?" In his book, *What You're Really Meant to Do*, Kaplan proposes that each of us has unique skills and abilities. Why then, he asks, would we try to mimic others or try to fit into someone else's definition of success?

One way to keep striving to realise your potential is to continually create a future that is bigger than your past, as Ted does. Of course, if it is a future doing what you love and making a difference, then you are well on the way.

Are you realising your potential?

By continually asking yourself this question, you will edge steadily closer to being both successful and happy.

Are you successful and happy?

Ivan was a perfectionist. This served him well for much of his career. People were impressed with the results he produced and he quickly moved into leadership roles. But now it seemed more like a curse. He was working long hours and was not fulfilled by his work. His health was suffering. His team found him demanding and impatient. But the thing that really irritated him was that he was now making predictable commitments to reduce his fear of failure. Playing a small game was inconsistent with his commitment to making a difference.

Ivan realised that being a perfectionist was not serving him. To be always striving for a perfect outcome was counterproductive. More often than not, an 80 per cent outcome delivered quickly on a stretch objective is better than procrastinating because we have not yet found a perfect solution.

He knew that a characteristic of game-changing leaders is the ability to commit to and achieve stretch results and elicit big commitments from those around them. So he reframed his perfectionism into the pursuit of excellence. He still has high standards but is now able to celebrate his and others' accomplishments. Like many of us, Ivan had focused on the expectation gap — that is, the gap between what we actually accomplish and what we expected to achieve. In Ivan's case, he always expected a perfect outcome so he was never satisfied.

Ivan began the practice of recording his accomplishments, big and small. He also instituted acknowledgement sessions with his team to ensure they knew they were appreciated and valued. The difference was like night and day. People now enjoy being around him, and bigger results are showing up. Even his wife says she has never seen him so relaxed.

> **"It's not because things are difficult that we dare not venture. It's because we dare not venture that they are difficult."**
> – Seneca –

Researchers from the Harvard Business School have found that people who were both successful and happy over the long term structured their activities around four major needs, and that lasting fulfilment comes when we pursue activities that address all four of these needs. The four needs were:

- **Happiness**: They pursued activities that produced pleasure and satisfaction.

- **Achievement**: They pursued activities that got tangible results.

- **Significance**: They pursued activities that made a positive impact on the people who matter most.

- **Legacy**: They pursued activities through which they could pass on their values and knowledge to others.

Which area could you increase your focus on?

TEN

Be your own coach

If you are hungry to put some of the ideas in this book into practice, here are some activities that will help you to be your own coach. Of course, they are no substitute for the real thing!

Is this the magic ingredient?

It's the late 1980s, a Friday night. I have not long been divorced and it's my alternate weekend with my three children, aged ten, eight and six years old.

As they pile into the car, I ask them, "What do you want this weekend to be about?" Craig says, "How about we go for ten times more excitement than we have ever had!" Kirsty and Bob immediately agree, "Yeah, that would be amazing!" they agree. The theme for the weekend is set.

It was our usual practice on each access weekend to set up a different theme. Invariably, whenever we did, it turned out great. When we occasionally didn't set it up, we got what we got. Nothing wrong, the weekend just tended to lack something.

We realised there was a profound difference between saying what was going to happen and reporting on what had happened to us. We all learned that if we set the theme first, then we were on the lookout to fit our weekend activities into our chosen theme.

A drive to a basketball match, for example, became an opportunity for an experience that was ten times more exciting than usual. Of course, it did not escape my children or me that if we could do it for a weekend, we could do it for the week, month or the whole year for that matter.

The beginning of the year is a perfect time to create a theme for the year. Here are some steps to creating your theme for the year.

1. Come up with a few possible themes to inspire you. Remember, your theme is not a reaction to what you did not like about last year, but a creative declaration of what you want this year

2. List your projects and objectives for the first half of the year

3. List your projects and objectives for the second half of the year

4. Look for patterns that connect the projects and objectives with your theme

5. Create your vision for the year, beginning with the end in mind

6. Each week look for opportunities to fit your projects, tasks and personal interactions into your theme

7. Set up a daily process to record your "wins"

8. Schedule a meeting with yourself at the end of each quarter to acknowledge how you are going with your theme. Change it if you think of something better

Here are some examples of themes I have heard of:

- Hell yeah! [or no!]
- Buckle up
- Smashing down barriers
- Being world class
- Commitment with a sense of urgency
- Reinvention
- Going first class
- Finding my authentic voice.

What is a theme that would be the magic ingredient for you?

Where are you now on the influence curve?

And where do you need to be, given the challenges you face?

Remember, the way to get results through using this model is to *put it into practice*. You could read the book from cover to cover and then to put it down and say okay, I've got all that. But the book is designed around a coaching program we have used successfully with hundreds of people. The coaching model mixes theory and practice, which the research shows is how we learn best.

The first thing to do is to think about where you are now on the influence curve. But it is not like you do it once and that is it. You may have just started a new role and be at the *position* stage. Perhaps in your previous role you were at the top of the curve, at the *service* stage. Maybe you get a new boss and start all over again. The environment may change or you take on a big project, which changes where you now find yourself. Review the stages of the influence curve in Part 2 of the book and determine where you are now and where you need to be.

What challenges do you face now? Notice I am not talking about building your influence so you can apply it one day in the distant future. I mean expanding your influence to meet a big challenge you face *right now*. It's okay if you are struggling with that. In the next activity, I'll explain how to create a stretch objective so you can turn the idea from a nice theory into concrete reality.

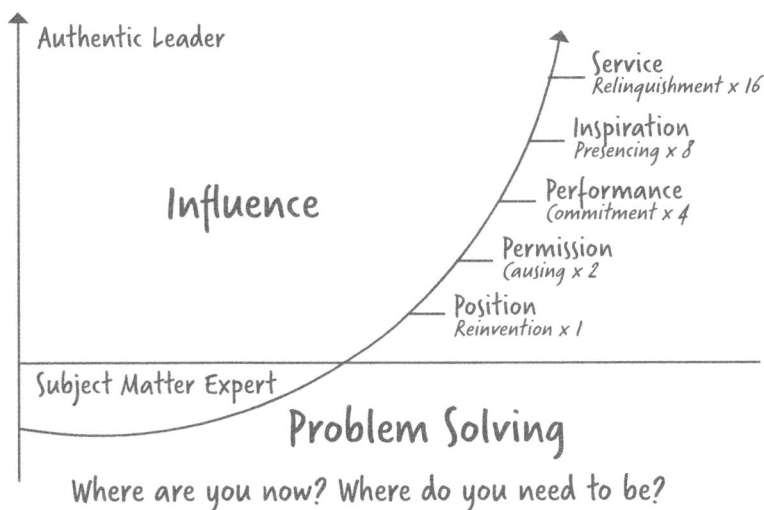

Authentic Leader

Influence

Service
Relinquishment x 16

Inspiration
Presencing x 8

Performance
Commitment x 4

Permission
Causing x 2

Position
Reinvention x 1

Subject Matter Expert

Problem Solving
Where are you now? Where do you need to be?

Figure 15: Where are you on the influence curve?

Creating the BIG game

Now we will create a "game" with a specific and measurable stretch objective to be achieved over the next three to six months. The game needs to be both a stretch commitment and something that inspires you. The best place to start is to focus on something you are passionate about. For example, some clients have created a big game to turn around a poisonous customer relationship. Others have taken on a major change program that their part of the business needs to introduce. Or perhaps you may have a big project that has gone off the rails and you want to get it back on track. It may be that your department's internal stakeholder relationships are not as good as they could be and you want to set an objective to turn this situation around.

Other stretch objectives I have seen include:

- gaining agreement for the business case for an upgrade to a legacy system
- selling a digital strategy to the executive leadership team
- getting a new strategy approved by senior management
- presenting a streamlined process for forecasting and setting business priorities.

The reason I am emphasising that it is best to choose a topic you are passionate about is simple. If the objective you set is big enough, at some point you may wonder why you were crazy enough to set it in the first place. At that point, you can reconnect with your passion for the topic to keep you going. If, on the other hand, you are uninspired, then the big commitment you set will end up being something you simply procrastinate over or do while all the time resenting it. Similarly, even if it is an objective that inspires you, without a stretch commitment you are likely to end up frustrated because you will not be making the difference you know you could make.

INSPIRED

Frustration

Big Game

UNCOMMITED————————COMMITED

Procrastination

Resentment

UNINSPIRED

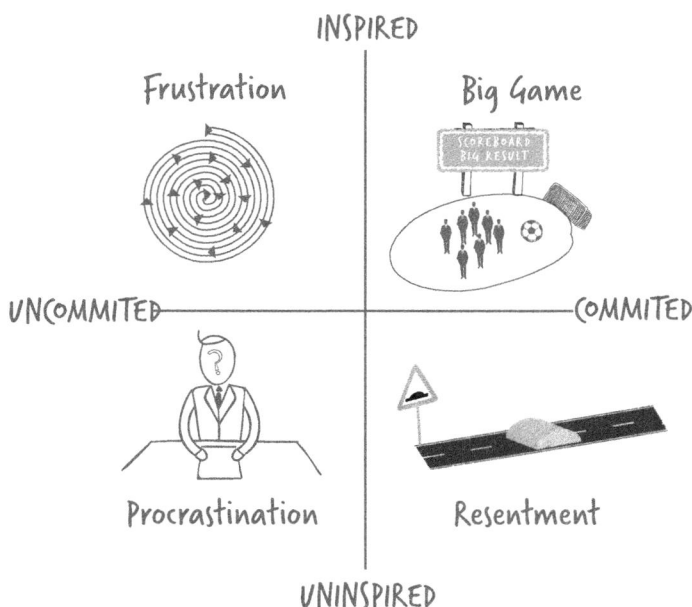

Figure 16: Creating a BIG game

Specific and measurable results

Notice that the examples we listed in the previous activity are of a specific character. They are not mere concepts, like "improve client relationships" or "get better at presentations". Your stretch objective needs to have a specific and measurable result — that is, something needs to be delivered within a specific timeframe. The more specific you can make it the better. We have found that a three to six-month timeframe is ideal. That could mean you are targeting a significant milestone in a larger project that goes beyond that timeframe. But three to six months is suitable for an objective with a sense of immediacy.

Setting a twelve-month objective generally leads to the impression that there is plenty of time to get around to it. The other part of being specific is that the result needs to be achieved by an agreed date (such as 30 June this year), rather than in a generalised timeframe, such as "in the first half of the year" or "over the next six months or so".

We can use some of the previous examples to illustrate the point about making the objective specific:

- Gaining agreement for the business case for an upgrade to a legacy system — the CFO signs off and approves the budget by 30 June, six months from now.

- Selling a digital strategy to the executive leadership team — the executive leadership team endorse the strategy at their offsite meeting on 31 March, three months from now.

- Getting a new strategy for your area of accountability approved by senior management — your stakeholders have all endorsed the strategy and your boss has approved it by 30 September.

- Presenting a streamlined process for forecasting and setting business priorities — the executive leadership team approve the process you recommend at their monthly meeting on 1 February.

Note we suggest you set a *stretch* objective. It needs to be something that looks unachievable to you today. Remember, our contention in this book is that game-changing leaders make big commitments that appear impossible at the time they make them. So if you already know you can achieve your objective, then it is not big enough. There is nothing wrong with that, but a stretch objective requires you to find a new level in your leadership. That is how you move up the influence curve. Once you declare the game you are playing, you should be on the edge of your chair.

The game will take into account the key issues you face and your leadership aspirations. These may include the following:

- What are the key elements of the 'game' — who, what, by when (specific measurable results)?

- What is the context for the game — what outcomes are you creating with the game?

- Who are you 'being' — what leadership qualities do you need to fulfil this game?

- Are there role models you wish to emulate?

- Who are the team members who will support you to win the game?

- What other resources are available to you?

- What are the milestones for the game?

- Create a scoreboard — how will you measure the progress and success of your game?

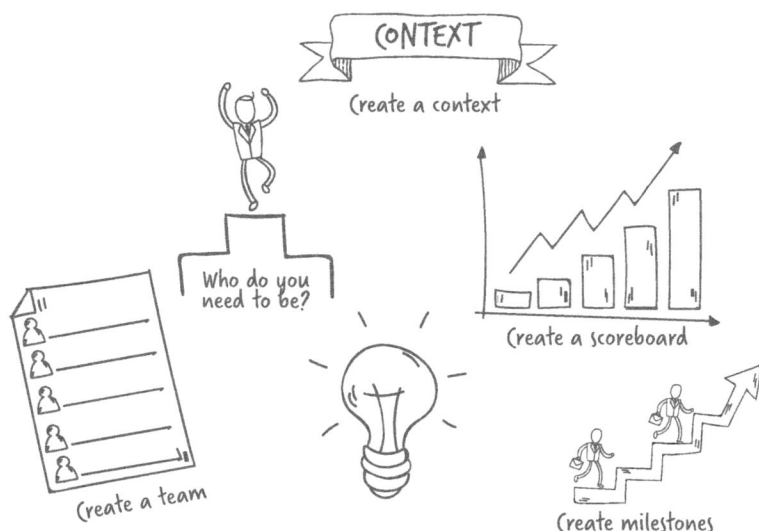

Figure 17: Creating the game

Begin with the end in mind

Has your vision for the year turned out as you had hoped? Not the company's, but your own personal vision. You may not have written it down, but you probably had a picture in mind of your personal and professional objectives for this year. Maybe you thought it was time to get out from under the day-to-day pressures and take your career in a new direction. Perhaps you wanted to implement a big new strategy. Whatever your objectives were, you may be either celebrating your success or lamenting the fact that nothing much has changed this year.

We routinely visualise what we want in other areas of our lives. If you have ever built or purchased a home you will have had a picture in your mind of what you wanted. It might have included the number of bedrooms, the location, the price range and many other particulars. Maybe you have imagined an exciting holiday. Or you may have visualised what success would look like before commencing a big project.

In *The 7 Habits of Highly Effective People*, Stephen R. Covey recommends that we "Begin with the end in mind": first we create a mental picture of what things will look like, then we take action to fulfil this objective.

A personal vision begins with the end in mind. Tania wrote down her vision for the next twelve months, which was to realise her dream to secure a global opportunity. She was specific about the things that were important to her. She envisaged plenty of autonomy in a global role, being professionally stretched and making something brand new happen. At first she was sceptical that she could achieve such bold objectives. But she put them down anyway, and to her great surprise it all turned out much sooner than she had expected.

There is something powerful about writing down a personal vision. One way to do it is to write it as a letter from the future — for example, dated twelve months out. You simply describe what you see, hear and feel as though it has already happened. Part of Tania's vision was, "I am in a great new global role, working with an energised team making something brand new happen." The more specific you can be the better. That means putting aside your concern about how it will happen. It may not all turn out just because you write it down. But it is more likely to come about if you spend some time clarifying your personal vision.

What is your personal vision for the next twelve months?

Here are some guidelines for writing your personal vision. Write a letter to yourself or someone in your life, dated twelve months out, outlining your vision. Write the letter in the first person "I". Remember that it is written in the present tense as though you are describing what has already turned out:

- What are you seeing, doing, hearing, feeling?
- What results are showing up?
- What had to happen to get you here?
- What leadership qualities did you need to achieve it?
- What is your area of "thought leadership" and how have you become recognised for it?
- Who do you now know yourself to be?
- What is your experience of yourself?
- What are your daily practices?
- What does your calendar look like?
- How do others around you experience you?
- What difference does it make in the world?

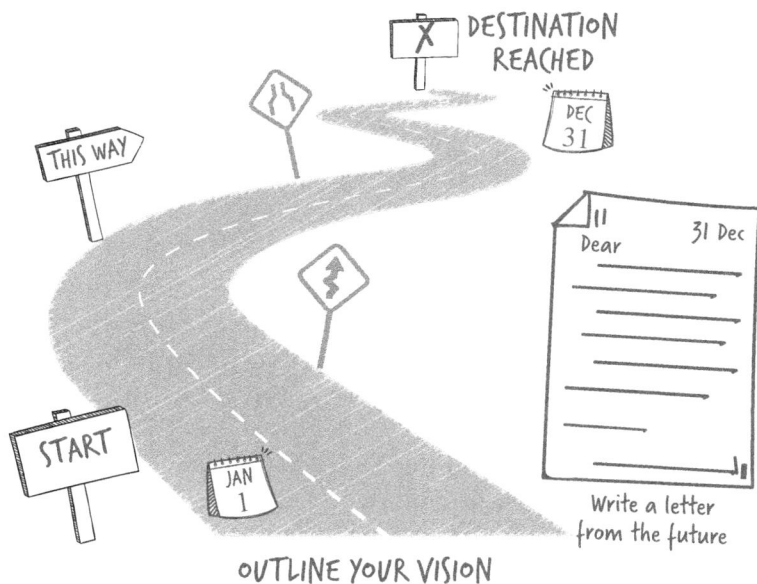

Figure 18: Begin with the end in mind

Reinvent your strength

How do you discover what your inherent strength is? You may have your own insights, but you really want to understand how others perceive your strength. Why? Well, it's one thing for you to tell yourself what your strength is, but unless others perceive that strength, you may as well say it does not really exist.

For example, a client of mine received some feedback that he did not have sufficient business skills. So he did an MBA and built up these skills, but they still claimed he lacked business skills! What he failed to understand was that he had not managed the *perception* that others had of him.

143

The following activity will help you to discover your strength.

Find three to five people who will be both direct and constructive in their feedback. Be careful to choose people who can do both. Some find it difficult to be direct in their feedback. They will tell you, "Oh no, I can't think of anything you could improve on." Other people will tell you, "Ah yes, I've been wanting to tell you this for a long time," and will use the opportunity to settle an old score. The feedback needs to be constructive to be valuable.

Here are some questions to ask in your strength and weakness interviews:

- What are my strengths?
- What are my weaknesses?
- What can you count on me for?
- What can you not count on me for?
- What does everyone know about me?

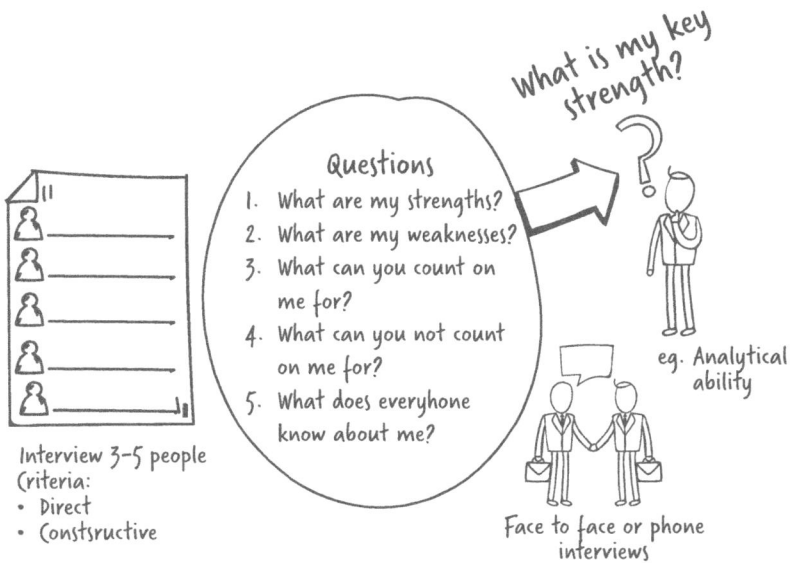

Figure 19: Strengths and weaknesses interviews

Your aim is to identify a key strength from these interviews — not a technical skill, like database management or solutions architect, but an inherent strength that runs like a thread throughout your career. It is a transferable strength. For example, your key strength may be analytical ability or a can-do, action-oriented strength. Or it may be connecting with people and forming relationships based on mutual trust.

The objective is to take your key strength, whatever it is, to a whole new level, while also identifying any associated weakness.

Here are a few examples.

Strength	Weakness
Analytical ability	Analysis paralysis
Can-do	Taking on too much
People and relationships	Wanting to be liked
Problem solving	Solving the small problems instead of the strategic issues

Having identified your key strength, you can now take it to a new level. This is an opportunity to *redefine* your key strength for yourself. In the process, you can develop your own personal charter, which we discussed in chapter 4.

Looking forward, here are some questions to guide your thinking about redefining your key strength and creating your personal charter. It is important to note that we are talking about how your key strength looks from here, not how it may have looked in the past. You are truly *reinventing* it.

- What is my strength and how could I reinvent it?
- What is my experience as I use my key strength?
- What do others experience when I am using my strength?
- What difference does my strength make in the world?

- As I use my strength, what would I be doing, saying and feeling, and what would be happening around me?

- What daily practices do I have to utilise more of my strength?

- What does my calendar look like as I reinvent my strength?

- What will I stop doing?

- What practices do I utilise when my strength becomes a weakness?

- What conversations could I end to use more of my key strength?

- What conversations could I start to use more of my key strength?

- What can I be counted on for?

- What do I stand for?

It's all people and it's all relationships

"The problem is with Accounts," I said. It was early in my career and I was telling my boss why our purchasing proposal was stalled. I was worked up about how "Accounts" were making our life difficult. He asked me a couple of times who the problem was with, but I was not listening.

Finally, in exasperation he asked, "But who? What is their name?"

"Oh, it's Bill," I responded.

"Right, let's think about Bill and what he wants," my boss said. "There is no such thing as Accounts; organisations are just a collection of people. It's all people and it's all relationships," he said. "We need to think about Bill and what's in it for him to agree to what we want."

Once we considered Bill and put our proposal in terms that were relevant to him, he became our partner instead of an adversary. To my surprise and delight he quickly approved the revised version. It was a valuable life lesson.

We have all done it; used a one-size-fits-all approach to our stakeholders. We use the generic slide pack that we presented to our boss to try to convince other stakeholders to support our proposal. But individual people are at the heart of every big objective. Each stakeholder will view our proposal through their own lens.

You may need to bring your team on board to support you. Perhaps you have to influence your key clients or your strategic suppliers. Each stakeholder needs a targeted approach if you want to bring people along with you.

It also seems that what we say first is critically important in winning them over. That is the point that Robert Cialdini, makes in his latest book, *Pre-Suasion*. Dr Cialdini has spent much of his career researching the science of influence. He argues that what you say first changes the way people experience what you present to them later. For example, asking your boss to provide advice on a plan, rather than to give their *opinions* or *expectations* regarding it, puts them in a cooperative state of mind before they even experience the proposal. That makes them more favourable to it when they later encounter it.

Whatever your current game-changing objective is, you will need to bring your key stakeholders along with you. It may be your manager or perhaps the team that you need to support you. It may be your key clients or your strategic suppliers. You will need a stakeholder plan to successfully bring people along with you.

Make a list of the key stakeholders whom you depend on for the success of your stretch objective.

Here is an approach that I have used with many clients over the years to help them to clarify their objective with each stakeholder and to craft their communication specifically for that target audience.

Who specifically is your audience?

Naming that person will focus your mind on them. Let's say it is Max.

What is your specific aim?

The more specific you can be the better. One way to clarify your outcome is to list what you will see, hear and feel if you achieve your aim. For example, you might decide that you will see your boss leading a discussion to endorse your proposal. You hear him arguing that we need this initiative to take us into the future. You feel a sense of excitement among the management team as they become convinced that your proposal is exactly what they have been looking for. Remember, your intended outcome will vary with each stakeholder. In this example, you want Max to endorse your proposal at the steering committee meeting next week.

What's in it for each audience member to give you what you want?

Find something that will motivate that individual to give you what you want. If you are familiar with Maslow's hierarchy of needs, you are looking for motivators low down in the pyramid. Self-esteem and recognition by others is a critical motivator for most people in leadership roles. Max, in this case, may be motivated by getting his KPIs achieved.

What is the message?

Your message needs to tap into your audience's motivation. Imagine you bumped into one of your stakeholders in the street and he said, "I haven't read your proposal yet. Just tell me what it's all about." What is the short and punchy version of your message that encapsulates it? It is not the only thing you will say on the topic. You may have lots more to back up your summary. But this is the message you want to leave your stakeholder with. For example, "Max, approving this proposal next week will help double your group's results in six months."

What is the best method to reach your audience?

Have you noticed that people absorb information quite differently? Some are more persuaded by the big picture while others tend to focus on the details? Some like the formal approach of a meeting in their office, with an outline of your proposal in front of them. Some may prefer that you draw a visual representation on a whiteboard.

Another stakeholder may opt for the informal approach of discussing your proposal over a coffee. Choose whatever works best for the stakeholder you are trying to reach. It is not a one-size-fits-all situation. Let's say Max is informal and would like to see a one-page summary: you can meet over a coffee to show him your diagram.

How could you better target your communication with your key stakeholders?

Commitment and opportunities

Remember, as a game-changing leader you are making big commitments to make things happen that were not going to happen by themselves. So, all the little commitments, all the small promises and requests along the way, add up to the accomplishment of the big commitment. When you step over the small promise to get the report done by an agreed date, because it doesn't really matter all that much, you are effectively diminishing your big promise to change the game.

There are two parts to this assignment. The first part gives you access to the "action" activity that follows on how to make requests and elicit powerful promises from those around you. Second, if you are expecting others to deliver on their commitments, then you had better make sure you do what you said you would do.

Keeping your promise, doing what you said you would do when you said you would do it, is the foundation stone for all our work, for without it the game cannot move forward. Always honour your word, and communicate when for any reason you are not able to keep your promise. It is valuable to create a record of all your promises and requests.

Remember the red Toyota syndrome, when you decide to buy a certain type of car, and suddenly you see the very same car everywhere? Similarly, you will find that once you have set your stretch objective you will discover many opportunities to push it forward.

There are two types of opportunities to capture: those that exist already and need only to be seized, and those you specifically create.

Here are some examples of existing opportunities that clients have used to forward their game:

- Present an agenda item at the executive leadership team strategic offsite

- Ask for a slot to present a specific call to action at a regular weekly management meeting

- Make time to see an important stakeholder who is visiting your office

- Offer to fix a problem encountered by a key stakeholder that your objective solves

- Speak at a staff update about how your objective advances your vision

- Present at a networking event on your topic and seek lessons from a wider network

Here are some examples of opportunities that my clients have created to forward their game:

- Identify stakeholders who could help create a demand for my objective

- A stakeholder who has just been appointed into a new role could build on my agenda to help make his or her mark

- Interview people in the marketplace and leverage my findings with a paper and a talk. (Refer to Frances's example in "Create opportunities to change the game" in chapter 6)

- Invite key stakeholders to a forum to address our strategic challenge, and establish a process for keeping them in the loop

- Invite an external "expert" to help get my message across and build greater awareness on an issue related to my objective

- Bring in people from other geographies, industries or areas who have experience with a challenge related to the one we face to share their insights

Action

One way to create high-performing leaders around you is to challenge them with a stretch objective. If you believe they have what it takes, then you know they will expand their leadership capability.

Paying it forward is not entirely an altruistic idea. In his book, *Give and Take: Why helping others drives our success,* Adam Grant distinguishes the givers from the takers and matchers. Grant's research shows that of the three groups, it is the givers who end up ahead in the long run.

Could you believe in someone more than they believe in themselves?

There are many ways you could cause other leaders to step up their leadership. One is to challenge them with a stretch objective, something that will take them out of their comfort zone. You know that if they take on the challenge they will find some capability they didn't know they had.

You can also encourage more leadership by making more requests — that is, you can set a specific results target by a specific time and hold people accountable for achieving those results. An exercise that builds muscle in this is to take on a new practice of making requests of others around you at least five times per day over the next six weeks.

The requests may be directed to people above, below or sideways from you, but in each case, they need to provide the person with a leadership opportunity. A simple example could be to ask a team member to act as your delegate by attending a meeting that you would normally attend. A larger request might be to ask someone to take on a big project that is off the rails and get it back on track.

You could make a request upwards for your manager to come and address your team on his or her priorities or vision. The overriding requirement is that your request provide others with a leadership opportunity. You get to be the judge of what constitutes a leadership opportunity.

A request needs to be specific and measurable. It is not a request when we talk in generalities about the project that's off the rails with one of our direct reports and leave them with a statement along the lines of, "Well I'll be interested to hear what you think." They will not be clear what you're looking for and you should not be surprised if you do not get a satisfactory response.

A more specific request could be, "Could you give me a one-page report analysing the problems we face and your recommendations on what we should do about them, and could you get it to me by 5.00 p.m. on Wednesday please." Now the recipient of the request has three options: (1) they can accept your request, (2) they can decline your request, or (3) they can make a counter-offer. For example, a counter-offer could be, "I can't achieve the 5.00 p.m. Wednesday deadline, but I could get it to you by midday on Thursday." You then have the same options (accept, decline or counter-offer).

Arguably, an old client of mine doubled the size of his business through adopting this simple practice. Stephen was in charge of new products and had been in the firing line from his boss and his business colleagues for not delivering on his commitments. Stephen thought his boss did not understand the pressures he had to deal with. He felt like a circus clown trying to keep several spinning plates from crashing down.

To his credit, he realised the impact that he was having on people around him and the damage he was causing to his personal brand. He had not been aware that people felt they could not count on him and that it was only a matter of time before they avoided dealing with him. It stunned him into action.

He realised that if he operated with integrity, then he would not find himself having to offer excuses after the event. People would see him as someone who took his commitments seriously. He agreed that he needed to be in communication the moment he knew a commitment looked like slipping so he could renegotiate the due date. This was a huge breakthrough for Stephen. He rebuilt trust with his stakeholders because of the clarity he was now providing.

Stephen adopted the practice of using "what by when" every day. Emails to his team contained the time and date for a deliverable in the subject line. His business unit colleagues began to trust him and became his advocates. They sought additional funding to support more product development because of their newfound faith in him.

It did not end there. Customers purchased more products because reliability went up. Arguably Stephen's practice of focusing on 'what by when' made such a difference to the business that is has effectively doubled in size.

One thing you will quickly begin to realise if you follow Stephen's example is that the more requests you make of people and the more promises they make to you, the more you need a good system to capture them. You need a way to track and monitor these requests and promises. In my own experience, and watching other leaders, I have found that each time the size of the game increases, you need to find a new way to manage your commitments.

You need a system that tracks your projects, tasks and meetings and, importantly, the promises other people make you. I'm not prescriptive about the kind of system you should use. There are plenty of good books and applications that will help you manage your time and commitments. The important point is to have some way of recording the requests you make and the promises others make to you. Trying to carry it all in your head is a big mistake.

Each working day for the next two weeks, make five powerful requests that provide leadership opportunities for others, and record the promises that people make you.

The power of acknowledgement

Accomplishing game-changing objectives is like digging for gemstones. You have to go deep to find the treasure. We all tend to resist acknowledgement of our accomplishments and to undervalue our achievements. When you have been playing a big game it is important, both for yourself and for those around you, to drill into what you have accomplished. You need to get past your resistance as well as theirs to acknowledge your accomplishments.

You may recognise the tendency to pass off a complimentary remark about what a great job you have done with a flippant response. You've seen people brush it off with a comment like, "Oh, it was nothing really. Anyone could have done it."

Have you come across people who are up to big things and accomplishing a lot, but never seem to be satisfied or fulfilled by what they do? Satisfaction and accomplishment go hand in hand. If you are playing a big game, you will not always achieve your objective, but you will have achieved far more than if you had not played big. Acknowledging your accomplishments along the way to achieving your objectives will give you a sense of satisfaction and fulfilment.

In her work on the broaden-and-build theory of positive emotions, Barbara Fredrickson suggests that "positive emotions are worth cultivating not just as end states in themselves but also as a means to achieving psychological growth and improved wellbeing over time".

This is sometimes a difficult conversation to have in Australia, where we don't like to see people getting above themselves. My mother always said, "Don't show off! No one likes a show-off." It took me a long time to realise that she was not saying don't be proud of yourself and don't be proud of what you have accomplished.

Graham had begun to influence his senior stakeholders to adopt a more comprehensive digital strategy, but he fell short of achieving the objective he had set himself. He had established a new governance forum for IT initiatives and eventually the IT strategy. He had also helped to break down the barriers between IT and the business. He acknowledged that he had accomplished quite a lot and had gone much further than he would have without setting a big objective like that.

One form of resistance to accomplishment that people often use is to say that they are not finished yet. But game-changing leaders are never done. They are always creating, moving on, expanding their leadership.

It is possible to complete each stage along the path to your stretch objective by acknowledging what you have accomplished. You will never get the satisfaction and fulfilment you seek if you wait until you are finished before acknowledging your accomplishments. Acknowledging your accomplishments is in itself a step towards completion.

In Daniel's case, he did not receive the acknowledgement he thought was due from his employer. In fact, quite the opposite, he failed to land the job he sought and there seemed to be some suggestion that he had not delivered on his boss's expectations. When he carried out his own self-assessment, however, he could see that he had accomplished quite a lot and that he had created a foundation that set him up for a great new job.

Completion, then, is our responsibility. When we are not willing to do the work of acknowledging our accomplishments, we put the responsibility back on others. But it's not their job, and we may wait a very long time for them to give us the acknowledgement we think is our due.

As a game-changing leader, you will also find that treating people with respect and giving them the appreciation they crave will make you a more effective leader. It makes a huge difference to people to get a heartfelt thank you and an expression of your gratitude for the work they have done.

The Appreciative Inquiry model has a lot to offer here. Essentially, it focuses on what works rather than on what doesn't. It's like watering the garden. Using this model, you can concentrate on the positive rather than devoting time to post-implementation reviews on what did not work or who is to blame for any failure. If you focus more on acknowledging what worked, you can do more of this and you are likely to go much further with your objective to change the game. In this you are like a business: in a business you are either going forward or backwards. Equilibrium is not an option.

Game-changing leaders continually create a new big game on the foundation of what they've accomplished. McKinsey found that four kinds of behaviours account for 89 per cent of leadership effectiveness. One key behaviour is operating with a strong results orientation. The report's authors conclude, "Leadership is about not only developing and communicating a vision and setting objectives, but also following through to achieve results."

This does not mean you should not look at what did not work in your big game. Proper acknowledgement provides an opportunity to look at what did not work from a powerful position. It is a gap to close rather than a failure by you or them. Elite athletes have no problem with looking at how they can constantly improve their performance to stay at the top.

Sometimes simply acknowledging what was not completed, without going into a long story about it, can provide a new opening for action. For example, at the end of the year Graham was acknowledging everything he had accomplished. Once again, for the fourth year in a row, he had not completed his PhD thesis, but rather than beating himself up about it, he simply acknowledged it, full stop. Without taking on the excess baggage of self-recrimination, he was more inspired to set an objective to complete it next year.

What comes next is therefore not a reaction to what didn't work. What's next is of your own creation, based on who you know yourself to be. It's about taking your strength to a new level.

Are you serving people around you?

Gary was a great role model for me of a leader who truly appreciated people. When he had received a deliverable that someone had promised him — a report or recommendation, say — he always made sure to thank them, and not just in a cursory way. He would sincerely convey his appreciation for the work they had done and the thought that had gone into it, while also recognising that they had had to fit it into their busy schedule. If something needed to be changed, then that could be more easily addressed once he had given them a full acknowledgement. People would go away glowing and would always go the extra mile for him.

Game-changing leaders treat people with respect and give them the appreciation we all crave. It is not all about being nice, though. They believe in the capabilities of their people and expect a big game from them. They appreciate them for who they really are and don't let them get away with anything less. In *Mindset*, Carol Dweck talks of the growth mindset as focusing on a passion for learning rather than a hunger for approval. This makes a huge difference.

We call this the *service* stage on the influence curve, where leaders multiply their influence through shifting their focus to those around them.

The idea of *servant leadership* is an ancient one that was brought back to life in Robert Greenleaf's seminal book, *The Power of Servant Leadership*. He realised that organisations that thrived had leaders who acted more as supportive coaches, serving the needs of both the employees and the organisation. As he puts it, "A servant-leader focuses primarily on the growth and well-being of people and the communities to which they belong. While traditional leadership generally involves the accumulation and exercise of power by one at the 'top of the pyramid', servant leadership is different. The servant-leader shares power, puts the needs of others first and helps people develop and perform as highly as possible."

Are you serving people around you?

Final thoughts

Actions speak louder than words

Thank you for reading this book. I hope it has given you some insights and ideas that you can use to expand your leadership. However great those insights may be though, the only thing that will make any real difference is *action*. No doubt, like me, you have seen many game-changing strategies that have gone nowhere because they were not accompanied by game-changing leadership. You have probably also been to a course or a conference and learned some interesting stuff and you have thought later, I must review those notes I took that are now sitting on a shelf somewhere. But you never quite get there.

This book will have real and lasting value only if you translate the ideas into action. Set a stretch objective to *make something big happen* in the next six months. The bigger and bolder the better. Get a team of people together who share your passion for the objective, and start taking action.

As you can tell, I am passionate about game-changing leadership and the difference it makes. Indeed, I firmly believe it is the key to every challenge we face in the world. The more we build our own leadership capability, as well as those around us, the more we will be able to solve some of the big problems we face.

Finally, paying it forward. When my niece Stephanie was 12 years old she was asked what leadership lessons she had learned from being school captain in her final year in primary school. Her answer was that it was the opportunity to give other people leadership opportunities so that they could be great leaders. It was an amazingly mature expression of the ultimate job of a leader, which is to create more leaders.

Stay in touch

I would love you to hear how you go applying the ideas in this book to build your leadership influence and change the game.

Please connect with me via my website, www.donovanleadership.com, where you can stay in touch by signing up for my regular leadership updates.

If there is anything I can do to help you or your organisation, please drop me a line. I provide one-on-one executive coaching programs and team facilitation programs to support leaders to change the game. I regularly speak to organisations and teams on the power of game-changing leadership.

You can email me at brian@donovanleadership.com.

Best regards,

Brian

About the author

Brian Donovan is an executive coach, facilitator, speaker and writer who has worked with numerous leaders and teams seeking to take their leadership to a new level. He has worked with leaders across a broad spectrum of industry sectors including IT, banking and finance, professional services, telecommunications, government, health and not-for-profit.

As the Director of Donovan Leadership, a business he created in 2007, Brian draws from his practical experience as a senior executive. He was the Chief Executive Officer of the IT Skills Hub from its inception in May 2001 until May 2005. The IT Skills Hub was a not-for-profit company formed by the Australian Government and twenty of the nation's leading ICT companies. During that period, he led a number of leading-edge research programs and leadership training initiatives.

Prior to this, Brian was General Manager, Corporate Affairs for Telstra's Network & Technology division. In this role, he was responsible for media and government relations as well as employee communications for up to 15,000 staff across the country. During his career Brian has worked in the telecommunications sector in a number of different roles, ranging from employee relations, industrial relations, project management and corporate affairs.

Brian founded Donovan Leadership to share his knowledge and passion. Since 2007, Donovan Leadership has been actively inspiring leaders to new heights, uncovering new perspectives to expand possibilities, and transforming technical specialists into successful leaders.

He has a passion for game-changing leadership and is energised by an ongoing program of research and scholarship. The impetus for this book was the main conclusion he drew from the latest Big Kahuna Leadership Survey: that companies that develop game-changing leadership capability will be better equipped to avoid the threat and capture the growth opportunities of digital and technology disruption.